This Journal Belongs to

_____

My Catholic Prayer Journal
ISBN-13: 978-1719144414
ISBN-10: 1719144419

Welcome!

This prayer journal requires minor instruction which you will find below. Please read this in order to get the most out of your journal.

You can start this journal at any month of the year, but please start at the beginning of a month. This journal is mainly made up of 3 parts:

1. MONTHLY PLANNING PAGES: Fill this out at the beginning of the month (with your spouse, if you're married) and start the month's journey to a deeper life in Christ. I recommend going back to the planning pages throughout the week to ensure you're on track to complete your goals. Just remember to make your goals attainable and be honest with yourself!

2. DAILY PRAYERS: The daily prayer pages are made up of the morning prayers (to be said first thing in the morning), Lectio Devina, and the Examen, The Lectio Devina section can be done anytime during the day. The journal will walk you through the steps. Start with the gospel reading for the day (find it at usccb.org) or a book in the Bible and set aside some uninterrupted time to let God speak to you through it. The last section in the daily prayers pages is the Examen which is based off of St. Ignatius of Loyola's Examen. The Examen should be done at the end of your day and it is, simply put, a reflection of your day in the presence of God. (And so important for spiritual growth!)

3. EXTRAS: Also in this journal you will find simple coloring pages, extra note pages at the end of each month, and questions to stimulate your mind and prayer life concerning your place in life through Mary's intercession and your vocations (found at the beginning of the journal).

Simply put, this journal should help you to "pray without ceasing."
1 Thessalonians 5:17

You can get free printables to use alongside this book at Catholicmommyblogs.com to assist your monthly planning and focus on the faith.

I hope this prayer journal assists in bringing you closer to Christ.

God Bless You,
Lis Luwia

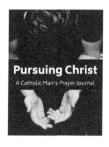

Pursuing Christ: A Catholic Man's Prayer Journal
Our Men's Prayer Journal is available on Amazon! Consider buying one for your dad, brother, or significant other.

A prayer journal for teen girls (Through the Lens of God) is coming soon! Sign up for our emails to stay updated.

Mary

Memorare to Our Blessed Mother

Remember, O most gracious Virgin Mary, that never was it known that anyone who fled to thy protection, implored thy help, or sought thine intercession was left unaided.

Inspired by this confidence, I fly unto thee, O Virgin of virgins, my mother; to thee do I come, before thee I stand, sinful and sorrowful. O Mother of the Word Incarnate, despise not my petitions, but in thy mercy hear and answer me. Amen.

WHO IS MARY TO YOU?

IN WHAT WAYS WOULD YOU LIKE TO EMULATE HER?

HOW WOULD EMULATING MARY CHANGE YOUR RELATIONSHIP WITH JESUS?

HOW WILL YOU MAKE ACTIVE STEPS TO GROW COSER TO MARY THIS YEAR?

Daughter

Jesus said, "Let the little children come to me, and do not stop them; for it is to such as these that the kingdom of heaven belongs." Matthew 19:14

LIST SOME WORDS THAT DESCRIBE WHAT KIND OF A DAUGHTER YOU ARE

HOW DO YOU SHARE YOUR FAITH WITH YOUR PARENTS AND SIBLINGS (& IN-LAWS)?

LIST WHO YOU WILL PRAY FOR AND HOW IN THIS COMING YEAR

HOW WILL YOU MAKE ACTIVE STEPS TO INFUSE THESE RELATIONSHIPS IN CHRIST?

Wife

"Though one may be overpowered, two can defend themselves. A cord of three strands is not quickly broken." Ecclesiastes 4:12

LIST SOME WORDS THAT DESCRIBE WHAT KIND OF A WIFE YOU ARE

HOW DO YOU SHARE YOUR FAITH WITH YOUR HUSBAND?

HOW WILL YOU SUPPORT YOUR HUSBAND SPIRITUALLY THIS YEAR?

SET ASIDE A SPECIAL TIME EVERY DAY AND PRAY FOR YOUR HUSBAND. HOW WILL YOU PRAY FOR HIM?

Mother

LIST SOME WORDS THAT DESCRIBE WHAT KIND OF A MOTHER YOU ARE

HOW DO YOU SHARE YOUR FAITH WITH YOUR FAMILY?

HOW WILL YOU SUPPORT YOUR CHILDREN'S SPIRITUAL GROWTH THIS YEAR?

FOR WHAT AND HOW WILL YOU PRAY FOR YOUR CHILDREN?

January

"The sweet Name of Jesus produces in us holy thoughts, fills the soul with noble sentiments, strengthens virtue, begets good works, and nourishes pure affection. All spiritual food leaves the soul dry, if it contain not that penetrating oil, the Name Jesus." - St. Bernard of Clairvaux

PERSONAL RESOLUTIONS

SPIRITUAL READING LOG

LAST CONFESSION DATE

HOLY ACTIVITIES WITH MY FAMILY/ FRIENDS

PRAYER REQUESTS

✔ ROSARY & CHAPLET TRACKER

"We are all called to be great saints; don't miss the opportunity!" - Mother Angelica

Day 1

O Jesus, through the Immaculate Heart of Mary, I offer You my prayers, works, joys and sufferings of this day for all the intentions of Your Sacred Heart, in union with the Holy Sacrifice of the Mass throughout the world, in reparation for my sins, for the intentions of all my relatives and friends, and in particular for the intentions of the Holy Father. Amen.

Lectio Devina

READ & WRITE IT OUT: BIBLE VERSE

REFLECT: WHAT DOES THIS MEAN TO ME?

RESPOND: WHAT DO I SAY TO GOD ABOUT THIS?

REST IN MEDITATION: HOW IS GOD ASKING ME TO CHANGE?

Examen

1. Ask God to see your day and actions through His eyes
2. Thank Him
3. Review and meditate on your day and actions
4. Face your shortcomings
5. Ask God for guidance and pray about tomorrow

I'M THANKFUL FOR...

MY SINS & SHORTCOMINGS TODAY

Day 2

Morning Prayer

O Jesus, through the Immaculate Heart of Mary, I offer You my prayers, works, joys and sufferings of this day for all the intentions of Your Sacred Heart, in union with the Holy Sacrifice of the Mass throughout the world, in reparation for my sins, for the intentions of all my relatives and friends, and in particular for the intentions of the Holy Father. Amen.

Lectio Devina

READ & WRITE IT: BIBLE VERSE

REFLECT: WHAT DOES THIS MEAN TO ME?

RESPOND: WHAT DO I SAY TO GOD ABOUT THIS?

REST IN MEDITATION: HOW IS GOD ASKING ME TO CHANGE?

Examen

1. Ask God to see your day and actions through His eyes
2. Thank Him
3. Review and meditate on your day and actions
4. Face your shortcomings
5. Ask God for guidance and pray about tomorrow

I'M THANKFUL FOR...

MY SINS & SHORTCOMINGS TODAY

Day 3   *Morning Prayer*

O Jesus, through the Immaculate Heart of Mary, I offer You my prayers, works, joys and sufferings of this day for all the intentions of Your Sacred Heart, in union with the Holy Sacrifice of the Mass throughout the world, in reparation for my sins, for the intentions of all my relatives and friends, and in particular for the intentions of the Holy Father. Amen.

READ & WRITE IT OUT: BIBLE VERSE

REFLECT: WHAT DOES THIS MEAN TO ME?

RESPOND: WHAT DO I SAY TO GOD ABOUT THIS?

REST IN MEDITATION: HOW IS GOD ASKING ME TO CHANGE?

Lectio Devina

1. Ask God to see your day and actions through His eyes
2. Thank Him
3. Review and meditate on your day and actions
4. Face your shortcomings
5. Ask God for guidance and pray about tomorrow

Examen

I'M THANKFUL FOR...

MY SINS & SHORTCOMINGS TODAY

Day 4   *Morning Prayer*

O Jesus, through the Immaculate Heart of Mary, I offer You my prayers, works, joys and sufferings of this day for all the intentions of Your Sacred Heart, in union with the Holy Sacrifice of the Mass throughout the world, in reparation for my sins, for the intentions of all my relatives and friends, and in particular for the intentions of the Holy Father. Amen.

READ & WRITE IT: BIBLE VERSE

REFLECT: WHAT DOES THIS MEAN TO ME?

RESPOND: WHAT DO I SAY TO GOD ABOUT THIS?

REST IN MEDITATION: HOW IS GOD ASKING ME TO CHANGE?

Lectio Devina

1. Ask God to see your day and actions through His eyes
2. Thank Him
3. Review and meditate on your day and actions
4. Face your shortcomings
5. Ask God for guidance and pray about tomorrow

Examen

I'M THANKFUL FOR...

MY SINS & SHORTCOMINGS TODAY

Day 5

O Jesus, through the Immaculate Heart of Mary, I offer You my prayers, works, joys and sufferings of this day for all the intentions of Your Sacred Heart, in union with the Holy Sacrifice of the Mass throughout the world, in reparation for my sins, for the intentions of all my relatives and friends, and in particular for the intentions of the Holy Father. Amen.

Lectio Devina

READ & WRITE IT OUT: BIBLE VERSE

REFLECT: WHAT DOES THIS MEAN TO ME?

RESPOND: WHAT DO I SAY TO GOD ABOUT THIS?

REST IN MEDITATION: HOW IS GOD ASKING ME TO CHANGE?

Examen

1. Ask God to see your day and actions through His eyes
2. Thank Him
3. Review and meditate on your day and actions
4. Face your shortcomings
5. Ask God for guidance and pray about tomorrow

I'M THANKFUL FOR...

MY SINS & SHORTCOMINGS TODAY

Day 6

Morning Prayer

O Jesus, through the Immaculate Heart of Mary, I offer You my prayers, works, joys and sufferings of this day for all the intentions of Your Sacred Heart, in union with the Holy Sacrifice of the Mass throughout the world, in reparation for my sins, for the intentions of all my relatives and friends, and in particular for the intentions of the Holy Father. Amen.

Lectio Devina

READ & WRITE IT: BIBLE VERSE

REFLECT: WHAT DOES THIS MEAN TO ME?

RESPOND: WHAT DO I SAY TO GOD ABOUT THIS?

REST IN MEDITATION: HOW IS GOD ASKING ME TO CHANGE?

Examen

1. Ask God to see your day and actions through His eyes
2. Thank Him
3. Review and meditate on your day and actions
4. Face your shortcomings
5. Ask God for guidance and pray about tomorrow

I'M THANKFUL FOR...

MY SINS & SHORTCOMINGS TODAY

Day 7

O Jesus, through the Immaculate Heart of Mary, I offer You my prayers, works, joys and sufferings of this day for all the intentions of Your Sacred Heart, in union with the Holy Sacrifice of the Mass throughout the world, in reparation for my sins, for the intentions of all my relatives and friends, and in particular for the intentions of the Holy Father. Amen.

Lectio Devina

READ & WRITE IT OUT: BIBLE VERSE

REFLECT: WHAT DOES THIS MEAN TO ME?

RESPOND: WHAT DO I SAY TO GOD ABOUT THIS?

REST IN MEDITATION: HOW IS GOD ASKING ME TO CHANGE?

Examen

1. Ask God to see your day and actions through His eyes
2. Thank Him
3. Review and meditate on your day and actions
4. Face your shortcomings
5. Ask God for guidance and pray about tomorrow

I'M THANKFUL FOR...

MY SINS & SHORTCOMINGS TODAY

Day 8

Morning Prayer

O Jesus, through the Immaculate Heart of Mary, I offer You my prayers, works, joys and sufferings of this day for all the intentions of Your Sacred Heart, in union with the Holy Sacrifice of the Mass throughout the world, in reparation for my sins, for the intentions of all my relatives and friends, and in particular for the intentions of the Holy Father. Amen.

Lectio Devina

READ & WRITE IT: BIBLE VERSE

REFLECT: WHAT DOES THIS MEAN TO ME?

RESPOND: WHAT DO I SAY TO GOD ABOUT THIS?

REST IN MEDITATION: HOW IS GOD ASKING ME TO CHANGE?

Examen

1. Ask God to see your day and actions through His eyes
2. Thank Him
3. Review and meditate on your day and actions
4. Face your shortcomings
5. Ask God for guidance and pray about tomorrow

I'M THANKFUL FOR...

MY SINS & SHORTCOMINGS TODAY

Day 9

O Jesus, through the Immaculate Heart of Mary, I offer You my prayers, works, joys and sufferings of this day for all the intentions of Your Sacred Heart, in union with the Holy Sacrifice of the Mass throughout the world, in reparation for my sins, for the intentions of all my relatives and friends, and in particular for the intentions of the Holy Father. Amen.

Lectio Devina

READ & WRITE IT OUT: BIBLE VERSE

REFLECT: WHAT DOES THIS MEAN TO ME?

RESPOND: WHAT DO I SAY TO GOD ABOUT THIS?

REST IN MEDITATION: HOW IS GOD ASKING ME TO CHANGE?

Examen

1. Ask God to see your day and actions through His eyes
2. Thank Him
3. Review and meditate on your day and actions
4. Face your shortcomings
5. Ask God for guidance and pray about tomorrow

I'M THANKFUL FOR...

MY SINS & SHORTCOMINGS TODAY

Day 10

Morning Prayer

O Jesus, through the Immaculate Heart of Mary, I offer You my prayers, works, joys and sufferings of this day for all the intentions of Your Sacred Heart, in union with the Holy Sacrifice of the Mass throughout the world, in reparation for my sins, for the intentions of all my relatives and friends, and in particular for the intentions of the Holy Father. Amen.

Lectio Devina

READ & WRITE IT: BIBLE VERSE

REFLECT: WHAT DOES THIS MEAN TO ME?

RESPOND: WHAT DO I SAY TO GOD ABOUT THIS?

REST IN MEDITATION: HOW IS GOD ASKING ME TO CHANGE?

Examen

1. Ask God to see your day and actions through His eyes
2. Thank Him
3. Review and meditate on your day and actions
4. Face your shortcomings
5. Ask God for guidance and pray about tomorrow

I'M THANKFUL FOR...

MY SINS & SHORTCOMINGS TODAY

Day 11

O Jesus, through the Immaculate Heart of Mary, I offer You my prayers, works, joys and sufferings of this day for all the intentions of Your Sacred Heart, in union with the Holy Sacrifice of the Mass throughout the world, in reparation for my sins, for the intentions of all my relatives and friends, and in particular for the intentions of the Holy Father. Amen.

Lectio Devina

READ & WRITE IT OUT: BIBLE VERSE

REFLECT: WHAT DOES THIS MEAN TO ME?

RESPOND: WHAT DO I SAY TO GOD ABOUT THIS?

REST IN MEDITATION: HOW IS GOD ASKING ME TO CHANGE?

Examen

1. Ask God to see your day and actions through His eyes
2. Thank Him
3. Review and meditate on your day and actions
4. Face your shortcomings
5. Ask God for guidance and pray about tomorrow

I'M THANKFUL FOR...

MY SINS & SHORTCOMINGS TODAY

Day 12

Morning Prayer

O Jesus, through the Immaculate Heart of Mary, I offer You my prayers, works, joys and sufferings of this day for all the intentions of Your Sacred Heart, in union with the Holy Sacrifice of the Mass throughout the world, in reparation for my sins, for the intentions of all my relatives and friends, and in particular for the intentions of the Holy Father. Amen.

Lectio Devina

READ & WRITE IT: BIBLE VERSE

REFLECT: WHAT DOES THIS MEAN TO ME?

RESPOND: WHAT DO I SAY TO GOD ABOUT THIS?

REST IN MEDITATION: HOW IS GOD ASKING ME TO CHANGE?

Examen

1. Ask God to see your day and actions through His eyes
2. Thank Him
3. Review and meditate on your day and actions
4. Face your shortcomings
5. Ask God for guidance and pray about tomorrow

I'M THANKFUL FOR...

MY SINS & SHORTCOMINGS TODAY

Day 13

O Jesus, through the Immaculate Heart of Mary, I offer You my prayers, works, joys and sufferings of this day for all the intentions of Your Sacred Heart, in union with the Holy Sacrifice of the Mass throughout the world, in reparation for my sins, for the intentions of all my relatives and friends, and in particular for the intentions of the Holy Father. Amen.

Lectio Devina

READ & WRITE IT OUT: BIBLE VERSE

REFLECT: WHAT DOES THIS MEAN TO ME?

RESPOND: WHAT DO I SAY TO GOD ABOUT THIS?

REST IN MEDITATION: HOW IS GOD ASKING ME TO CHANGE?

Examen

1. Ask God to see your day and actions through His eyes
2. Thank Him
3. Review and meditate on your day and actions
4. Face your shortcomings
5. Ask God for guidance and pray about tomorrow

I'M THANKFUL FOR...

MY SINS & SHORTCOMINGS TODAY

Day 14

Morning Prayer

O Jesus, through the Immaculate Heart of Mary, I offer You my prayers, works, joys and sufferings of this day for all the intentions of Your Sacred Heart, in union with the Holy Sacrifice of the Mass throughout the world, in reparation for my sins, for the intentions of all my relatives and friends, and in particular for the intentions of the Holy Father. Amen.

Lectio Devina

READ & WRITE IT: BIBLE VERSE

REFLECT: WHAT DOES THIS MEAN TO ME?

RESPOND: WHAT DO I SAY TO GOD ABOUT THIS?

REST IN MEDITATION: HOW IS GOD ASKING ME TO CHANGE?

Examen

1. Ask God to see your day and actions through His eyes
2. Thank Him
3. Review and meditate on your day and actions
4. Face your shortcomings
5. Ask God for guidance and pray about tomorrow

I'M THANKFUL FOR...

MY SINS & SHORTCOMINGS TODAY

Day 15

Morning Prayer

O Jesus, through the Immaculate Heart of Mary, I offer You my prayers, works, joys and sufferings of this day for all the intentions of Your Sacred Heart, in union with the Holy Sacrifice of the Mass throughout the world, in reparation for my sins, for the intentions of all my relatives and friends, and in particular for the intentions of the Holy Father. Amen.

Lectio Devina

READ & WRITE IT OUT: BIBLE VERSE

REFLECT: WHAT DOES THIS MEAN TO ME?

RESPOND: WHAT DO I SAY TO GOD ABOUT THIS?

REST IN MEDITATION: HOW IS GOD ASKING ME TO CHANGE?

Examen

1. Ask God to see your day and actions through His eyes
2. Thank Him
3. Review and meditate on your day and actions
4. Face your shortcomings
5. Ask God for guidance and pray about tomorrow

I'M THANKFUL FOR...

MY SINS & SHORTCOMINGS TODAY

Day 16

Morning Prayer

O Jesus, through the Immaculate Heart of Mary, I offer You my prayers, works, joys and sufferings of this day for all the intentions of Your Sacred Heart, in union with the Holy Sacrifice of the Mass throughout the world, in reparation for my sins, for the intentions of all my relatives and friends, and in particular for the intentions of the Holy Father. Amen.

Lectio Devina

READ & WRITE IT: BIBLE VERSE

REFLECT: WHAT DOES THIS MEAN TO ME?

RESPOND: WHAT DO I SAY TO GOD ABOUT THIS?

REST IN MEDITATION: HOW IS GOD ASKING ME TO CHANGE?

Examen

1. Ask God to see your day and actions through His eyes
2. Thank Him
3. Review and meditate on your day and actions
4. Face your shortcomings
5. Ask God for guidance and pray about tomorrow

I'M THANKFUL FOR...

MY SINS & SHORTCOMINGS TODAY

Day 17   *Morning Prayer*

O Jesus, through the Immaculate Heart of Mary, I offer You my prayers, works, joys and sufferings of this day for all the intentions of Your Sacred Heart, in union with the Holy Sacrifice of the Mass throughout the world, in reparation for my sins, for the intentions of all my relatives and friends, and in particular for the intentions of the Holy Father. Amen.

READ & WRITE IT OUT: BIBLE VERSE

REFLECT: WHAT DOES THIS MEAN TO ME?

RESPOND: WHAT DO I SAY TO GOD ABOUT THIS?

REST IN MEDITATION: HOW IS GOD ASKING ME TO CHANGE?

1. Ask God to see your day and actions through His eyes
2. Thank Him
3. Review and meditate on your day and actions
4. Face your shortcomings
5. Ask God for guidance and pray about tomorrow

I'M THANKFUL FOR...

MY SINS & SHORTCOMINGS TODAY

Day 18   *Morning Prayer*

O Jesus, through the Immaculate Heart of Mary, I offer You my prayers, works, joys and sufferings of this day for all the intentions of Your Sacred Heart, in union with the Holy Sacrifice of the Mass throughout the world, in reparation for my sins, for the intentions of all my relatives and friends, and in particular for the intentions of the Holy Father. Amen.

READ & WRITE IT: BIBLE VERSE

REFLECT: WHAT DOES THIS MEAN TO ME?

RESPOND: WHAT DO I SAY TO GOD ABOUT THIS?

REST IN MEDITATION: HOW IS GOD ASKING ME TO CHANGE?

1. Ask God to see your day and actions through His eyes
2. Thank Him
3. Review and meditate on your day and actions
4. Face your shortcomings
5. Ask God for guidance and pray about tomorrow

I'M THANKFUL FOR...

MY SINS & SHORTCOMINGS TODAY

Lectio Devina

Examen

Day 19

Morning Prayer

O Jesus, through the Immaculate Heart of Mary, I offer You my prayers, works, joys and sufferings of this day for all the intentions of Your Sacred Heart, in union with the Holy Sacrifice of the Mass throughout the world, in reparation for my sins, for the intentions of all my relatives and friends, and in particular for the intentions of the Holy Father. Amen.

Lectio Devina

READ & WRITE IT OUT: BIBLE VERSE

REFLECT: WHAT DOES THIS MEAN TO ME?

RESPOND: WHAT DO I SAY TO GOD ABOUT THIS?

REST IN MEDITATION: HOW IS GOD ASKING ME TO CHANGE?

Examen

1. Ask God to see your day and actions through His eyes
2. Thank Him
3. Review and meditate on your day and actions
4. Face your shortcomings
5. Ask God for guidance and pray about tomorrow

I'M THANKFUL FOR...

MY SINS & SHORTCOMINGS TODAY

Day 20

Morning Prayer

O Jesus, through the Immaculate Heart of Mary, I offer You my prayers, works, joys and sufferings of this day for all the intentions of Your Sacred Heart, in union with the Holy Sacrifice of the Mass throughout the world, in reparation for my sins, for the intentions of all my relatives and friends, and in particular for the intentions of the Holy Father. Amen.

Lectio Devina

READ & WRITE IT: BIBLE VERSE

REFLECT: WHAT DOES THIS MEAN TO ME?

RESPOND: WHAT DO I SAY TO GOD ABOUT THIS?

REST IN MEDITATION: HOW IS GOD ASKING ME TO CHANGE?

Examen

1. Ask God to see your day and actions through His eyes
2. Thank Him
3. Review and meditate on your day and actions
4. Face your shortcomings
5. Ask God for guidance and pray about tomorrow

I'M THANKFUL FOR...

MY SINS & SHORTCOMINGS TODAY

Day 21

Morning Prayer

O Jesus, through the Immaculate Heart of Mary, I offer You my prayers, works, joys and sufferings of this day for all the intentions of Your Sacred Heart, in union with the Holy Sacrifice of the Mass throughout the world, in reparation for my sins, for the intentions of all my relatives and friends, and in particular for the intentions of the Holy Father. Amen.

READ & WRITE IT OUT: BIBLE VERSE

Lectio Devina

REFLECT: WHAT DOES THIS MEAN TO ME?

RESPOND: WHAT DO I SAY TO GOD ABOUT THIS?

REST IN MEDITATION: HOW IS GOD ASKING ME TO CHANGE?

Examen

1. Ask God to see your day and actions through His eyes
2. Thank Him
3. Review and meditate on your day and actions
4. Face your shortcomings
5. Ask God for guidance and pray about tomorrow

I'M THANKFUL FOR...

MY SINS & SHORTCOMINGS TODAY

Day 22

Morning Prayer

O Jesus, through the Immaculate Heart of Mary, I offer You my prayers, works, joys and sufferings of this day for all the intentions of Your Sacred Heart, in union with the Holy Sacrifice of the Mass throughout the world, in reparation for my sins, for the intentions of all my relatives and friends, and in particular for the intentions of the Holy Father. Amen.

READ & WRITE IT: BIBLE VERSE

Lectio Devina

REFLECT: WHAT DOES THIS MEAN TO ME?

RESPOND: WHAT DO I SAY TO GOD ABOUT THIS?

REST IN MEDITATION: HOW IS GOD ASKING ME TO CHANGE?

Examen

1. Ask God to see your day and actions through His eyes
2. Thank Him
3. Review and meditate on your day and actions
4. Face your shortcomings
5. Ask God for guidance and pray about tomorrow

I'M THANKFUL FOR...

MY SINS & SHORTCOMINGS TODAY

Day 23   *Morning Prayer*

O Jesus, through the Immaculate Heart of Mary, I offer You my prayers, works, joys and sufferings of this day for all the intentions of Your Sacred Heart, in union with the Holy Sacrifice of the Mass throughout the world, in reparation for my sins, for the intentions of all my relatives and friends, and in particular for the intentions of the Holy Father. Amen.

READ & WRITE IT OUT: BIBLE VERSE

REFLECT: WHAT DOES THIS MEAN TO ME?

RESPOND: WHAT DO I SAY TO GOD ABOUT THIS?

REST IN MEDITATION: HOW IS GOD ASKING ME TO CHANGE?

Lectio Devina

1. Ask God to see your day and actions through His eyes
2. Thank Him
3. Review and meditate on your day and actions
4. Face your shortcomings
5. Ask God for guidance and pray about tomorrow

I'M THANKFUL FOR...   MY SINS & SHORTCOMINGS TODAY

Examen

Day 24   *Morning Prayer*

O Jesus, through the Immaculate Heart of Mary, I offer You my prayers, works, joys and sufferings of this day for all the intentions of Your Sacred Heart, in union with the Holy Sacrifice of the Mass throughout the world, in reparation for my sins, for the intentions of all my relatives and friends, and in particular for the intentions of the Holy Father. Amen.

READ & WRITE IT: BIBLE VERSE

REFLECT: WHAT DOES THIS MEAN TO ME?

RESPOND: WHAT DO I SAY TO GOD ABOUT THIS?

REST IN MEDITATION: HOW IS GOD ASKING ME TO CHANGE?

Lectio Devina

1. Ask God to see your day and actions through His eyes
2. Thank Him
3. Review and meditate on your day and actions
4. Face your shortcomings
5. Ask God for guidance and pray about tomorrow

I'M THANKFUL FOR...   MY SINS & SHORTCOMINGS TODAY

Examen

Day 25   *Morning Prayer*

O Jesus, through the Immaculate Heart of Mary, I offer You my prayers, works, joys and sufferings of this day for all the intentions of Your Sacred Heart, in union with the Holy Sacrifice of the Mass throughout the world, in reparation for my sins, for the intentions of all my relatives and friends, and in particular for the intentions of the Holy Father. Amen.

READ & WRITE IT OUT: BIBLE VERSE

REFLECT: WHAT DOES THIS MEAN TO ME?

RESPOND: WHAT DO I SAY TO GOD ABOUT THIS?

REST IN MEDITATION: HOW IS GOD ASKING ME TO CHANGE?

Lectio Devina

1. Ask God to see your day and actions through His eyes
2. Thank Him
3. Review and meditate on your day and actions
4. Face your shortcomings
5. Ask God for guidance and pray about tomorrow

I'M THANKFUL FOR...

MY SINS & SHORTCOMINGS TODAY

Examen

Day 26   *Morning Prayer*

O Jesus, through the Immaculate Heart of Mary, I offer You my prayers, works, joys and sufferings of this day for all the intentions of Your Sacred Heart, in union with the Holy Sacrifice of the Mass throughout the world, in reparation for my sins, for the intentions of all my relatives and friends, and in particular for the intentions of the Holy Father. Amen.

READ & WRITE IT: BIBLE VERSE

REFLECT: WHAT DOES THIS MEAN TO ME?

RESPOND: WHAT DO I SAY TO GOD ABOUT THIS?

REST IN MEDITATION: HOW IS GOD ASKING ME TO CHANGE?

Lectio Devina

1. Ask God to see your day and actions through His eyes
2. Thank Him
3. Review and meditate on your day and actions
4. Face your shortcomings
5. Ask God for guidance and pray about tomorrow

I'M THANKFUL FOR...

MY SINS & SHORTCOMINGS TODAY

Examen

Day 27   *Morning Prayer*

O Jesus, through the Immaculate Heart of Mary, I offer You my prayers, works, joys and sufferings of this day for all the intentions of Your Sacred Heart, in union with the Holy Sacrifice of the Mass throughout the world, in reparation for my sins, for the intentions of all my relatives and friends, and in particular for the intentions of the Holy Father. Amen.

Lectio Devina

READ & WRITE IT OUT: BIBLE VERSE

REFLECT: WHAT DOES THIS MEAN TO ME?

RESPOND: WHAT DO I SAY TO GOD ABOUT THIS?

REST IN MEDITATION: HOW IS GOD ASKING ME TO CHANGE?

Examen

1. Ask God to see your day and actions through His eyes
2. Thank Him
3. Review and meditate on your day and actions
4. Face your shortcomings
5. Ask God for guidance and pray about tomorrow

I'M THANKFUL FOR...

MY SINS & SHORTCOMINGS TODAY

Day 28   *Morning Prayer*

O Jesus, through the Immaculate Heart of Mary, I offer You my prayers, works, joys and sufferings of this day for all the intentions of Your Sacred Heart, in union with the Holy Sacrifice of the Mass throughout the world, in reparation for my sins, for the intentions of all my relatives and friends, and in particular for the intentions of the Holy Father. Amen.

Lectio Devina

READ & WRITE IT: BIBLE VERSE

REFLECT: WHAT DOES THIS MEAN TO ME?

RESPOND: WHAT DO I SAY TO GOD ABOUT THIS?

REST IN MEDITATION: HOW IS GOD ASKING ME TO CHANGE?

Examen

1. Ask God to see your day and actions through His eyes
2. Thank Him
3. Review and meditate on your day and actions
4. Face your shortcomings
5. Ask God for guidance and pray about tomorrow

I'M THANKFUL FOR...

MY SINS & SHORTCOMINGS TODAY

Day 29

O Jesus, through the Immaculate Heart of Mary, I offer You my prayers, works, joys and sufferings of this day for all the intentions of Your Sacred Heart, in union with the Holy Sacrifice of the Mass throughout the world, in reparation for my sins, for the intentions of all my relatives and friends, and in particular for the intentions of the Holy Father. Amen.

Lectio Devina

READ & WRITE IT OUT: BIBLE VERSE

REFLECT: WHAT DOES THIS MEAN TO ME?

RESPOND: WHAT DO I SAY TO GOD ABOUT THIS?

REST IN MEDITATION: HOW IS GOD ASKING ME TO CHANGE?

Examen

1. Ask God to see your day and actions through His eyes
2. Thank Him
3. Review and meditate on your day and actions
4. Face your shortcomings
5. Ask God for guidance and pray about tomorrow

I'M THANKFUL FOR...

MY SINS & SHORTCOMINGS TODAY

Day 30

Morning Prayer

O Jesus, through the Immaculate Heart of Mary, I offer You my prayers, works, joys and sufferings of this day for all the intentions of Your Sacred Heart, in union with the Holy Sacrifice of the Mass throughout the world, in reparation for my sins, for the intentions of all my relatives and friends, and in particular for the intentions of the Holy Father. Amen.

Lectio Devina

READ & WRITE IT: BIBLE VERSE

REFLECT: WHAT DOES THIS MEAN TO ME?

RESPOND: WHAT DO I SAY TO GOD ABOUT THIS?

REST IN MEDITATION: HOW IS GOD ASKING ME TO CHANGE?

Examen

1. Ask God to see your day and actions through His eyes
2. Thank Him
3. Review and meditate on your day and actions
4. Face your shortcomings
5. Ask God for guidance and pray about tomorrow

I'M THANKFUL FOR...

MY SINS & SHORTCOMINGS TODAY

Day 31

O Jesus, through the Immaculate Heart of Mary, I offer You my prayers, works, joys and sufferings of this day for all the intentions of Your Sacred Heart, in union with the Holy Sacrifice of the Mass throughout the world, in reparation for my sins, for the intentions of all my relatives and friends, and in particular for the intentions of the Holy Father. Amen.

Lectio Devina

READ & WRITE IT OUT: BIBLE VERSE

REFLECT: WHAT DOES THIS MEAN TO ME?

RESPOND: WHAT DO I SAY TO GOD ABOUT THIS?

REST IN MEDITATION: HOW IS GOD ASKING ME TO CHANGE?

Examen

1. Ask God to see your day and actions through His eyes
2. Thank Him
3. Review and meditate on your day and actions
4. Face your shortcomings
5. Ask God for guidance and pray about tomorrow

I'M THANKFUL FOR...

MY SINS & SHORTCOMINGS TODAY

PRAYERS & REFLECTIONS ON YOUR SPIRITUAL JOURNEY THIS MONTH

February

"When I think of Christian homes, I like to imagine them as being full of the light and joy that was found in the home of the Holy Family."
-St. Josemaría Escrivá

PERSONAL RESOLUTIONS

SPIRITUAL READING LOG

LAST CONFESSION DATE

HOLY ACTIVITIES WITH MY FAMILY/ FRIENDS

PRAYER REQUESTS

ROSARY & CHAPLET TRACKER

"We are all called to be great saints; don't miss the opportunity!" - Mother Angelica

Day 1

Morning Prayer

O Jesus, through the Immaculate Heart of Mary, I offer You my prayers, works, joys and sufferings of this day for all the intentions of Your Sacred Heart, in union with the Holy Sacrifice of the Mass throughout the world, in reparation for my sins, for the intentions of all my relatives and friends, and in particular for the intentions of the Holy Father. Amen.

Lectio Devina

READ & WRITE IT OUT: BIBLE VERSE

REFLECT: WHAT DOES THIS MEAN TO ME?

RESPOND: WHAT DO I SAY TO GOD ABOUT THIS?

REST IN MEDITATION: HOW IS GOD ASKING ME TO CHANGE?

Examen

1. Ask God to see your day and actions through His eyes
2. Thank Him
3. Review and meditate on your day and actions
4. Face your shortcomings
5. Ask God for guidance and pray about tomorrow

I'M THANKFUL FOR...

MY SINS & SHORTCOMINGS TODAY

Day 2

Morning Prayer

O Jesus, through the Immaculate Heart of Mary, I offer You my prayers, works, joys and sufferings of this day for all the intentions of Your Sacred Heart, in union with the Holy Sacrifice of the Mass throughout the world, in reparation for my sins, for the intentions of all my relatives and friends, and in particular for the intentions of the Holy Father. Amen.

Lectio Devina

READ & WRITE IT: BIBLE VERSE

REFLECT: WHAT DOES THIS MEAN TO ME?

RESPOND: WHAT DO I SAY TO GOD ABOUT THIS?

REST IN MEDITATION: HOW IS GOD ASKING ME TO CHANGE?

Examen

1. Ask God to see your day and actions through His eyes
2. Thank Him
3. Review and meditate on your day and actions
4. Face your shortcomings
5. Ask God for guidance and pray about tomorrow

I'M THANKFUL FOR...

MY SINS & SHORTCOMINGS TODAY

Day 3

O Jesus, through the Immaculate Heart of Mary, I offer You my prayers, works, joys and sufferings of this day for all the intentions of Your Sacred Heart, in union with the Holy Sacrifice of the Mass throughout the world, in reparation for my sins, for the intentions of all my relatives and friends, and in particular for the intentions of the Holy Father. Amen.

Lectio Devina

READ & WRITE IT OUT: BIBLE VERSE

REFLECT: WHAT DOES THIS MEAN TO ME?

RESPOND: WHAT DO I SAY TO GOD ABOUT THIS?

REST IN MEDITATION: HOW IS GOD ASKING ME TO CHANGE?

Examen

1. Ask God to see your day and actions through His eyes
2. Thank Him
3. Review and meditate on your day and actions
4. Face your shortcomings
5. Ask God for guidance and pray about tomorrow

I'M THANKFUL FOR...

MY SINS & SHORTCOMINGS TODAY

Day 4

Morning Prayer

O Jesus, through the Immaculate Heart of Mary, I offer You my prayers, works, joys and sufferings of this day for all the intentions of Your Sacred Heart, in union with the Holy Sacrifice of the Mass throughout the world, in reparation for my sins, for the intentions of all my relatives and friends, and in particular for the intentions of the Holy Father. Amen.

Lectio Devina

READ & WRITE IT: BIBLE VERSE

REFLECT: WHAT DOES THIS MEAN TO ME?

RESPOND: WHAT DO I SAY TO GOD ABOUT THIS?

REST IN MEDITATION: HOW IS GOD ASKING ME TO CHANGE?

Examen

1. Ask God to see your day and actions through His eyes
2. Thank Him
3. Review and meditate on your day and actions
4. Face your shortcomings
5. Ask God for guidance and pray about tomorrow

I'M THANKFUL FOR...

MY SINS & SHORTCOMINGS TODAY

Day 5   *Morning Prayer*

O Jesus, through the Immaculate Heart of Mary, I offer You my prayers, works, joys and sufferings of this day for all the intentions of Your Sacred Heart, in union with the Holy Sacrifice of the Mass throughout the world, in reparation for my sins, for the intentions of all my relatives and friends, and in particular for the intentions of the Holy Father. Amen.

READ & WRITE IT OUT: BIBLE VERSE

REFLECT: WHAT DOES THIS MEAN TO ME?

RESPOND: WHAT DO I SAY TO GOD ABOUT THIS?

REST IN MEDITATION: HOW IS GOD ASKING ME TO CHANGE?

Lectio Devina

1. Ask God to see your day and actions through His eyes
2. Thank Him
3. Review and meditate on your day and actions
4. Face your shortcomings
5. Ask God for guidance and pray about tomorrow

I'M THANKFUL FOR...

MY SINS & SHORTCOMINGS TODAY

Examen

Day 6   *Morning Prayer*

O Jesus, through the Immaculate Heart of Mary, I offer You my prayers, works, joys and sufferings of this day for all the intentions of Your Sacred Heart, in union with the Holy Sacrifice of the Mass throughout the world, in reparation for my sins, for the intentions of all my relatives and friends, and in particular for the intentions of the Holy Father. Amen.

READ & WRITE IT: BIBLE VERSE

REFLECT: WHAT DOES THIS MEAN TO ME?

RESPOND: WHAT DO I SAY TO GOD ABOUT THIS?

REST IN MEDITATION: HOW IS GOD ASKING ME TO CHANGE?

Lec-io Devina

1. Ask God to see your day and actions through His eyes
2. Thank Him
3. Review and meditate on your day and actions
4. Face your shortcomings
5. Ask God for guidance and pray about tomorrow

I'M THANKFUL FOR...

MY SINS & SHORTCOMINGS TODAY

Examen

Day 7

Morning Prayer

O Jesus, through the Immaculate Heart of Mary, I offer You my prayers, works, joys and sufferings of this day for all the intentions of Your Sacred Heart, in union with the Holy Sacrifice of the Mass throughout the world, in reparation for my sins, for the intentions of all my relatives and friends, and in particular for the intentions of the Holy Father. Amen.

READ & WRITE IT OUT: BIBLE VERSE

REFLECT: WHAT DOES THIS MEAN TO ME?

RESPOND: WHAT DO I SAY TO GOD ABOUT THIS?

REST IN MEDITATION: HOW IS GOD ASKING ME TO CHANGE?

Lectio Devina

1. Ask God to see your day and actions through His eyes
2. Thank Him
3. Review and meditate on your day and actions
4. Face your shortcomings
5. Ask God for guidance and pray about tomorrow

I'M THANKFUL FOR...

MY SINS & SHORTCOMINGS TODAY

Examen

Day 8

Morning Prayer

O Jesus, through the Immaculate Heart of Mary, I offer You my prayers, works, joys and sufferings of this day for all the intentions of Your Sacred Heart, in union with the Holy Sacrifice of the Mass throughout the world, in reparation for my sins, for the intentions of all my relatives and friends, and in particular for the intentions of the Holy Father. Amen.

READ & WRITE IT: BIBLE VERSE

REFLECT: WHAT DOES THIS MEAN TO ME?

RESPOND: WHAT DO I SAY TO GOD ABOUT THIS?

REST IN MEDITATION: HOW IS GOD ASKING ME TO CHANGE?

Lectio Devina

1. Ask God to see your day and actions through His eyes
2. Thank Him
3. Review and meditate on your day and actions
4. Face your shortcomings
5. Ask God for guidance and pray about tomorrow

I'M THANKFUL FOR...

MY SINS & SHORTCOMINGS TODAY

Examen

Day 9   *Morning Prayer*

O Jesus, through the Immaculate Heart of Mary, I offer You my prayers, works, joys and sufferings of this day for all the intentions of Your Sacred Heart, in union with the Holy Sacrifice of the Mass throughout the world, in reparation for my sins, for the intentions of all my relatives and friends, and in particular for the intentions of the Holy Father. Amen.

READ & WRITE IT OUT: BIBLE VERSE

Lectio Devina

REFLECT: WHAT DOES THIS MEAN TO ME?

RESPOND: WHAT DO I SAY TO GOD ABOUT THIS?

REST IN MEDITATION: HOW IS GOD ASKING ME TO CHANGE?

Examen

1. Ask God to see your day and actions through His eyes
2. Thank Him
3. Review and meditate on your day and actions
4. Face your shortcomings
5. Ask God for guidance and pray about tomorrow

I'M THANKFUL FOR...   MY SINS & SHORTCOMINGS TODAY

Day 10   *Morning Prayer*

O Jesus, through the Immaculate Heart of Mary, I offer You my prayers, works, joys and sufferings of this day for all the intentions of Your Sacred Heart, in union with the Holy Sacrifice of the Mass throughout the world, in reparation for my sins, for the intentions of all my relatives and friends, and in particular for the intentions of the Holy Father. Amen.

READ & WRITE IT: BIBLE VERSE

Lectio Devina

REFLECT: WHAT DOES THIS MEAN TO ME?

RESPOND: WHAT DO I SAY TO GOD ABOUT THIS?

REST IN MEDITATION: HOW IS GOD ASKING ME TO CHANGE?

Examen

1. Ask God to see your day and actions through His eyes
2. Thank Him
3. Review and meditate on your day and actions
4. Face your shortcomings
5. Ask God for guidance and pray about tomorrow

I'M THANKFUL FOR...   MY SINS & SHORTCOMINGS TODAY

Day 11

Morning Prayer

O Jesus, through the Immaculate Heart of Mary, I offer You my prayers, works, joys and sufferings of this day for all the intentions of Your Sacred Heart, in union with the Holy Sacrifice of the Mass throughout the world, in reparation for my sins, for the intentions of all my relatives and friends, and in particular for the intentions of the Holy Father. Amen.

Lectio Devina

READ & WRITE IT OUT: BIBLE VERSE

REFLECT: WHAT DOES THIS MEAN TO ME?

RESPOND: WHAT DO I SAY TO GOD ABOUT THIS?

REST IN MEDITATION: HOW IS GOD ASKING ME TO CHANGE?

Examen

1. Ask God to see your day and actions through His eyes
2. Thank Him
3. Review and meditate on your day and actions
4. Face your shortcomings
5. Ask God for guidance and pray about tomorrow

I'M THANKFUL FOR...

MY SINS & SHORTCOMINGS TODAY

Day 12

Morning Prayer

O Jesus, through the Immaculate Heart of Mary, I offer You my prayers, works, joys and sufferings of this day for all the intentions of Your Sacred Heart, in union with the Holy Sacrifice of the Mass throughout the world, in reparation for my sins, for the intentions of all my relatives and friends, and in particular for the intentions of the Holy Father. Amen.

Lectio Devina

READ & WRITE IT: BIBLE VERSE

REFLECT: WHAT DOES THIS MEAN TO ME?

RESPOND: WHAT DO I SAY TO GOD ABOUT THIS?

REST IN MEDITATION: HOW IS GOD ASKING ME TO CHANGE?

Examen

1. Ask God to see your day and actions through His eyes
2. Thank Him
3. Review and meditate on your day and actions
4. Face your shortcomings
5. Ask God for guidance and pray about tomorrow

I'M THANKFUL FOR...

MY SINS & SHORTCOMINGS TODAY

Day 13

O Jesus, through the Immaculate Heart of Mary, I offer You my prayers, works, joys and sufferings of this day for all the intentions of Your Sacred Heart, in union with the Holy Sacrifice of the Mass throughout the world, in reparation for my sins, for the intentions of all my relatives and friends, and in particular for the intentions of the Holy Father. Amen.

Lectio Devina

READ & WRITE IT OUT: BIBLE VERSE

REFLECT: WHAT DOES THIS MEAN TO ME?

RESPOND: WHAT DO I SAY TO GOD ABOUT THIS?

REST IN MEDITATION: HOW IS GOD ASKING ME TO CHANGE?

Examen

1. Ask God to see your day and actions through His eyes
2. Thank Him
3. Review and meditate on your day and actions
4. Face your shortcomings
5. Ask God for guidance and pray about tomorrow

I'M THANKFUL FOR...

MY SINS & SHORTCOMINGS TODAY

Day 14

Morning Prayer

O Jesus, through the Immaculate Heart of Mary, I offer You my prayers, works, joys and sufferings of this day for all the intentions of Your Sacred Heart, in union with the Holy Sacrifice of the Mass throughout the world, in reparation for my sins, for the intentions of all my relatives and friends, and in particular for the intentions of the Holy Father. Amen.

Lectio Devina

READ & WRITE IT: BIBLE VERSE

REFLECT: WHAT DOES THIS MEAN TO ME?

RESPOND: WHAT DO I SAY TO GOD ABOUT THIS?

REST IN MEDITATION: HOW IS GOD ASKING ME TO CHANGE?

Examen

1. Ask God to see your day and actions through His eyes
2. Thank Him
3. Review and meditate on your day and actions
4. Face your shortcomings
5. Ask God for guidance and pray about tomorrow

I'M THANKFUL FOR...

MY SINS & SHORTCOMINGS TODAY

Day 15

O Jesus, through the Immaculate Heart of Mary, I offer You my prayers, works, joys and sufferings of this day for all the intentions of Your Sacred Heart, in union with the Holy Sacrifice of the Mass throughout the world, in reparation for my sins, for the intentions of all my relatives and friends, and in particular for the intentions of the Holy Father. Amen.

READ & WRITE IT OUT: BIBLE VERSE

REFLECT: WHAT DOES THIS MEAN TO ME?

RESPOND: WHAT DO I SAY TO GOD ABOUT THIS?

REST IN MEDITATION: HOW IS GOD ASKING ME TO CHANGE?

Lectio Devina

1. Ask God to see your day and actions through His eyes
2. Thank Him
3. Review and meditate on your day and actions
4. Face your shortcomings
5. Ask God for guidance and pray about tomorrow

I'M THANKFUL FOR...

MY SINS & SHORTCOMINGS TODAY

Examen

Day 16

Morning Prayer

O Jesus, through the Immaculate Heart of Mary, I offer You my prayers, works, joys and sufferings of this day for all the intentions of Your Sacred Heart, in union with the Holy Sacrifice of the Mass throughout the world, in reparation for my sins, for the intentions of all my relatives and friends, and in particular for the intentions of the Holy Father. Amen.

READ & WRITE IT: BIBLE VERSE

REFLECT: WHAT DOES THIS MEAN TO ME?

RESPOND: WHAT DO I SAY TO GOD ABOUT THIS?

REST IN MEDITATION: HOW IS GOD ASKING ME TO CHANGE?

Lectio Devina

1. Ask God to see your day and actions through His eyes
2. Thank Him
3. Review and meditate on your day and actions
4. Face your shortcomings
5. Ask God for guidance and pray about tomorrow

I'M THANKFUL FOR...

MY SINS & SHORTCOMINGS TODAY

Examen

Day 17   *Morning Prayer*

O Jesus, through the Immaculate Heart of Mary, I offer You my prayers, works, joys and sufferings of this day for all the intentions of Your Sacred Heart, in union with the Holy Sacrifice of the Mass throughout the world, in reparation for my sins, for the intentions of all my relatives and friends, and in particular for the intentions of the Holy Father. Amen.

Lectio Devina

READ & WRITE IT OUT: BIBLE VERSE

REFLECT: WHAT DOES THIS MEAN TO ME?

RESPOND: WHAT DO I SAY TO GOD ABOUT THIS?

REST IN MEDITATION: HOW IS GOD ASKING ME TO CHANGE?

Examen

1. Ask God to see your day and actions through His eyes
2. Thank Him
3. Review and meditate on your day and actions
4. Face your shortcomings
5. Ask God for guidance and pray about tomorrow

I'M THANKFUL FOR...

MY SINS & SHORTCOMINGS TODAY

Day 18   *Morning Prayer*

O Jesus, through the Immaculate Heart of Mary, I offer You my prayers, works, joys and sufferings of this day for all the intentions of Your Sacred Heart, in union with the Holy Sacrifice of the Mass throughout the world, in reparation for my sins, for the intentions of all my relatives and friends, and in particular for the intentions of the Holy Father. Amen.

Lectio Devina

READ & WRITE IT: BIBLE VERSE

REFLECT: WHAT DOES THIS MEAN TO ME?

RESPOND: WHAT DO I SAY TO GOD ABOUT THIS?

REST IN MEDITATION: HOW IS GOD ASKING ME TO CHANGE?

Examen

1. Ask God to see your day and actions through His eyes
2. Thank Him
3. Review and meditate on your day and actions
4. Face your shortcomings
5. Ask God for guidance and pray about tomorrow

I'M THANKFUL FOR...

MY SINS & SHORTCOMINGS TODAY

Day 19

O Jesus, through the Immaculate Heart of Mary, I offer You my prayers, works, joys and sufferings of this day for all the intentions of Your Sacred Heart, in union with the Holy Sacrifice of the Mass throughout the world, in reparation for my sins, for the intentions of all my relatives and friends, and in particular for the intentions of the Holy Father. Amen.

Lectio Devina

READ & WRITE IT OUT: BIBLE VERSE

REFLECT: WHAT DOES THIS MEAN TO ME?

RESPOND: WHAT DO I SAY TO GOD ABOUT THIS?

REST IN MEDITATION: HOW IS GOD ASKING ME TO CHANGE?

Examen

1. Ask God to see your day and actions through His eyes
2. Thank Him
3. Review and meditate on your day and actions
4. Face your shortcomings
5. Ask God for guidance and pray about tomorrow

I'M THANKFUL FOR...

MY SINS & SHORTCOMINGS TODAY

Day 20

Morning Prayer

O Jesus, through the Immaculate Heart of Mary, I offer You my prayers, works, joys and sufferings of this day for all the intentions of Your Sacred Heart, in union with the Holy Sacrifice of the Mass throughout the world, in reparation for my sins, for the intentions of all my relatives and friends, and in particular for the intentions of the Holy Father. Amen.

Lectio Devina

READ & WRITE IT: BIBLE VERSE

REFLECT: WHAT DOES THIS MEAN TO ME?

RESPOND: WHAT DO I SAY TO GOD ABOUT THIS?

REST IN MEDITATION: HOW IS GOD ASKING ME TO CHANGE?

Examen

1. Ask God to see your day and actions through His eyes
2. Thank Him
3. Review and meditate on your day and actions
4. Face your shortcomings
5. Ask God for guidance and pray about tomorrow

I'M THANKFUL FOR...

MY SINS & SHORTCOMINGS TODAY

Day 21

O Jesus, through the Immaculate Heart of Mary, I offer You my prayers, works, joys and sufferings of this day for all the intentions of Your Sacred Heart, in union with the Holy Sacrifice of the Mass throughout the world, in reparation for my sins, for the intentions of all my relatives and friends, and in particular for the intentions of the Holy Father. Amen.

Lectio Devina

READ & WRITE IT OUT: BIBLE VERSE

REFLECT: WHAT DOES THIS MEAN TO ME?

RESPOND: WHAT DO I SAY TO GOD ABOUT THIS?

REST IN MEDITATION: HOW IS GOD ASKING ME TO CHANGE?

Examen

1. Ask God to see your day and actions through His eyes
2. Thank Him
3. Review and meditate on your day and actions
4. Face your shortcomings
5. Ask God for guidance and pray about tomorrow

I'M THANKFUL FOR...

MY SINS & SHORTCOMINGS TODAY

Day 22

Morning Prayer

O Jesus, through the Immaculate Heart of Mary, I offer You my prayers, works, joys and sufferings of this day for all the intentions of Your Sacred Heart, in union with the Holy Sacrifice of the Mass throughout the world, in reparation for my sins, for the intentions of all my relatives and friends, and in particular for the intentions of the Holy Father. Amen.

Lectio Devina

READ & WRITE IT: BIBLE VERSE

REFLECT: WHAT DOES THIS MEAN TO ME?

RESPOND: WHAT DO I SAY TO GOD ABOUT THIS?

REST IN MEDITATION: HOW IS GOD ASKING ME TO CHANGE?

Examen

1. Ask God to see your day and actions through His eyes
2. Thank Him
3. Review and meditate on your day and actions
4. Face your shortcomings
5. Ask God for guidance and pray about tomorrow

I'M THANKFUL FOR...

MY SINS & SHORTCOMINGS TODAY

Day 23

O Jesus, through the Immaculate Heart of Mary, I offer You my prayers, works, joys and sufferings of this day for all the intentions of Your Sacred Heart, in union with the Holy Sacrifice of the Mass throughout the world, in reparation for my sins, for the intentions of all my relatives and friends, and in particular for the intentions of the Holy Father. Amen.

Lectio Devina

READ & WRITE IT OUT: BIBLE VERSE

REFLECT: WHAT DOES THIS MEAN TO ME?

RESPOND: WHAT DO I SAY TO GOD ABOUT THIS?

REST IN MEDITATION: HOW IS GOD ASKING ME TO CHANGE?

Examen

1. Ask God to see your day and actions through His eyes
2. Thank Him
3. Review and meditate on your day and actions
4. Face your shortcomings
5. Ask God for guidance and pray about tomorrow

I'M THANKFUL FOR...

MY SINS & SHORTCOMINGS TODAY

Day 24

Morning Prayer

O Jesus, through the Immaculate Heart of Mary, I offer You my prayers, works, joys and sufferings of this day for all the intentions of Your Sacred Heart, in union with the Holy Sacrifice of the Mass throughout the world, in reparation for my sins, for the intentions of all my relatives and friends, and in particular for the intentions of the Holy Father. Amen.

Lectio Devina

READ & WRITE IT: BIBLE VERSE

REFLECT: WHAT DOES THIS MEAN TO ME?

RESPOND: WHAT DO I SAY TO GOD ABOUT THIS?

REST IN MEDITATION: HOW IS GOD ASKING ME TO CHANGE?

Examen

1. Ask God to see your day and actions through His eyes
2. Thank Him
3. Review and meditate on your day and actions
4. Face your shortcomings
5. Ask God for guidance and pray about tomorrow

I'M THANKFUL FOR...

MY SINS & SHORTCOMINGS TODAY

Day 25   *Morning Prayer*

O Jesus, through the Immaculate Heart of Mary, I offer You my prayers, works, joys and sufferings of this day for all the intentions of Your Sacred Heart, in union with the Holy Sacrifice of the Mass throughout the world, in reparation for my sins, for the intentions of all my relatives and friends, and in particular for the intentions of the Holy Father. Amen.

Lectio Devina

READ & WRITE IT OUT: BIBLE VERSE

REFLECT: WHAT DOES THIS MEAN TO ME?

RESPOND: WHAT DO I SAY TO GOD ABOUT THIS?

REST IN MEDITATION: HOW IS GOD ASKING ME TO CHANGE?

Examen

1. Ask God to see your day and actions through His eyes
2. Thank Him
3. Review and meditate on your day and actions
4. Face your shortcomings
5. Ask God for guidance and pray about tomorrow

I'M THANKFUL FOR...

MY SINS & SHORTCOMINGS TODAY

Day 26   *Morning Prayer*

O Jesus, through the Immaculate Heart of Mary, I offer You my prayers, works, joys and sufferings of this day for all the intentions of Your Sacred Heart, in union with the Holy Sacrifice of the Mass throughout the world, in reparation for my sins, for the intentions of all my relatives and friends, and in particular for the intentions of the Holy Father. Amen.

Lec-io Devina

READ & WRITE IT: BIBLE VERSE

REFLECT: WHAT DOES THIS MEAN TO ME?

RESPOND: WHAT DO I SAY TO GOD ABOUT THIS?

REST IN MEDITATION: HOW IS GOD ASKING ME TO CHANGE?

Examen

1. Ask God to see your day and actions through His eyes
2. Thank Him
3. Review and meditate on your day and actions
4. Face your shortcomings
5. Ask God for guidance and pray about tomorrow

I'M THANKFUL FOR...

MY SINS & SHORTCOMINGS TODAY

Day 27

O Jesus, through the Immaculate Heart of Mary, I offer You my prayers, works, joys and sufferings of this day for all the intentions of Your Sacred Heart, in union with the Holy Sacrifice of the Mass throughout the world, in reparation for my sins, for the intentions of all my relatives and friends, and in particular for the intentions of the Holy Father. Amen.

Lectio Devina

READ & WRITE IT OUT: BIBLE VERSE

REFLECT: WHAT DOES THIS MEAN TO ME?

RESPOND: WHAT DO I SAY TO GOD ABOUT THIS?

REST IN MEDITATION: HOW IS GOD ASKING ME TO CHANGE?

Examen

1. Ask God to see your day and actions through His eyes
2. Thank Him
3. Review and meditate on your day and actions
4. Face your shortcomings
5. Ask God for guidance and pray about tomorrow

I'M THANKFUL FOR...

MY SINS & SHORTCOMINGS TODAY

Day 28

Morning Prayer

O Jesus, through the Immaculate Heart of Mary, I offer You my prayers, works, joys and sufferings of this day for all the intentions of Your Sacred Heart, in union with the Holy Sacrifice of the Mass throughout the world, in reparation for my sins, for the intentions of all my relatives and friends, and in particular for the intentions of the Holy Father. Amen.

Lectio Devina

READ & WRITE IT: BIBLE VERSE

REFLECT: WHAT DOES THIS MEAN TO ME?

RESPOND: WHAT DO I SAY TO GOD ABOUT THIS?

REST IN MEDITATION: HOW IS GOD ASKING ME TO CHANGE?

Examen

1. Ask God to see your day and actions through His eyes
2. Thank Him
3. Review and meditate on your day and actions
4. Face your shortcomings
5. Ask God for guidance and pray about tomorrow

I'M THANKFUL FOR...

MY SINS & SHORTCOMINGS TODAY

Jesus, I trust in You!

March

"Though thou hast recourse to many saints as thine intercessors, go specially to St. Joseph, for he has great power with God." -St. Teresa of Avila

PERSONAL RESOLUTIONS

SPIRITUAL READING LOG

LAST CONFESSION DATE

HOLY ACTIVITIES WITH MY FAMILY/ FRIENDS

PRAYER REQUESTS

ROSARY & CHAPLET TRACKER

"We are all called to be great saints; don't miss the opportunity!" - Mother Angelica

Day 1   *Morning Prayer*

O Jesus, through the Immaculate Heart of Mary, I offer You my prayers, works, joys and sufferings of this day for all the intentions of Your Sacred Heart, in union with the Holy Sacrifice of the Mass throughout the world, in reparation for my sins, for the intentions of all my relatives and friends, and in particular for the intentions of the Holy Father. Amen.

READ & WRITE IT OUT: BIBLE VERSE

REFLECT: WHAT DOES THIS MEAN TO ME?

RESPOND: WHAT DO I SAY TO GOD ABOUT THIS?

REST IN MEDITATION: HOW IS GOD ASKING ME TO CHANGE?

Lectio Devina

1. Ask God to see your day and actions through His eyes
2. Thank Him
3. Review and meditate on your day and actions
4. Face your shortcomings
5. Ask God for guidance and pray about tomorrow

I'M THANKFUL FOR...   MY SINS & SHORTCOMINGS TODAY

Examen

Day 2   *Morning Prayer*

O Jesus, through the Immaculate Heart of Mary, I offer You my prayers, works, joys and sufferings of this day for all the intentions of Your Sacred Heart, in union with the Holy Sacrifice of the Mass throughout the world, in reparation for my sins, for the intentions of all my relatives and friends, and in particular for the intentions of the Holy Father. Amen.

READ & WRITE IT: BIBLE VERSE

REFLECT: WHAT DOES THIS MEAN TO ME?

RESPOND: WHAT DO I SAY TO GOD ABOUT THIS?

REST IN MEDITATION: HOW IS GOD ASKING ME TO CHANGE?

Lectio Devina

1. Ask God to see your day and actions through His eyes
2. Thank Him
3. Review and meditate on your day and actions
4. Face your shortcomings
5. Ask God for guidance and pray about tomorrow

I'M THANKFUL FOR...   MY SINS & SHORTCOMINGS TODAY

Examen

Day 3

O Jesus, through the Immaculate Heart of Mary, I offer You my prayers, works, joys and sufferings of this day for all the intentions of Your Sacred Heart, in union with the Holy Sacrifice of the Mass throughout the world, in reparation for my sins, for the intentions of all my relatives and friends, and in particular for the intentions of the Holy Father. Amen.

Lectio Devina

READ & WRITE IT OUT: BIBLE VERSE

REFLECT: WHAT DOES THIS MEAN TO ME?

RESPOND: WHAT DO I SAY TO GOD ABOUT THIS?

REST IN MEDITATION: HOW IS GOD ASKING ME TO CHANGE?

Examen

1. Ask God to see your day and actions through His eyes
2. Thank Him
3. Review and meditate on your day and actions
4. Face your shortcomings
5. Ask God for guidance and pray about tomorrow

I'M THANKFUL FOR...

MY SINS & SHORTCOMINGS TODAY

Day 4

Morning Prayer

O Jesus, through the Immaculate Heart of Mary, I offer You my prayers, works, joys and sufferings of this day for all the intentions of Your Sacred Heart, in union with the Holy Sacrifice of the Mass throughout the world, in reparation for my sins, for the intentions of all my relatives and friends, and in particular for the intentions of the Holy Father. Amen.

Lectio Devina

READ & WRITE IT: BIBLE VERSE

REFLECT: WHAT DOES THIS MEAN TO ME?

RESPOND: WHAT DO I SAY TO GOD ABOUT THIS?

REST IN MEDITATION: HOW IS GOD ASKING ME TO CHANGE?

Examen

1. Ask God to see your day and actions through His eyes
2. Thank Him
3. Review and meditate on your day and actions
4. Face your shortcomings
5. Ask God for guidance and pray about tomorrow

I'M THANKFUL FOR...

MY SINS & SHORTCOMINGS TODAY

Day 5   *Morning Prayer*

O Jesus, through the Immaculate Heart of Mary, I offer You my prayers, works, joys and sufferings of this day for all the intentions of Your Sacred Heart, in union with the Holy Sacrifice of the Mass throughout the world, in reparation for my sins, for the intentions of all my relatives and friends, and in particular for the intentions of the Holy Father. Amen.

Lectio Devina

READ & WRITE IT OUT: BIBLE VERSE

REFLECT: WHAT DOES THIS MEAN TO ME?

RESPOND: WHAT DO I SAY TO GOD ABOUT THIS?

REST IN MEDITATION: HOW IS GOD ASKING ME TO CHANGE?

Examen

1. Ask God to see your day and actions through His eyes
2. Thank Him
3. Review and meditate on your day and actions
4. Face your shortcomings
5. Ask God for guidance and pray about tomorrow

I'M THANKFUL FOR...   MY SINS & SHORTCOMINGS TODAY

Day 6   *Morning Prayer*

O Jesus, through the Immaculate Heart of Mary, I offer You my prayers, works, joys and sufferings of this day for all the intentions of Your Sacred Heart, in union with the Holy Sacrifice of the Mass throughout the world, in reparation for my sins, for the intentions of all my relatives and friends, and in particular for the intentions of the Holy Father. Amen.

Lectio Devina

READ & WRITE IT: BIBLE VERSE

REFLECT: WHAT DOES THIS MEAN TO ME?

RESPOND: WHAT DO I SAY TO GOD ABOUT THIS?

REST IN MEDITATION: HOW IS GOD ASKING ME TO CHANGE?

Examen

1. Ask God to see your day and actions through His eyes
2. Thank Him
3. Review and meditate on your day and actions
4. Face your shortcomings
5. Ask God for guidance and pray about tomorrow

I'M THANKFUL FOR...   MY SINS & SHORTCOMINGS TODAY

Day 7   *Morning Prayer*

O Jesus, through the Immaculate Heart of Mary, I offer You my prayers, works, joys and sufferings of this day for all the intentions of Your Sacred Heart, in union with the Holy Sacrifice of the Mass throughout the world, in reparation for my sins, for the intentions of all my relatives and friends, and in particular for the intentions of the Holy Father. Amen.

READ & WRITE IT OUT: BIBLE VERSE

REFLECT: WHAT DOES THIS MEAN TO ME?

RESPOND: WHAT DO I SAY TO GOD ABOUT THIS?

REST IN MEDITATION: HOW IS GOD ASKING ME TO CHANGE?

Lectio Devina

1. Ask God to see your day and actions through His eyes
2. Thank Him
3. Review and meditate on your day and actions
4. Face your shortcomings
5. Ask God for guidance and pray about tomorrow

I'M THANKFUL FOR...

MY SINS & SHORTCOMINGS TODAY

Examen

Day 8   *Morning Prayer*

O Jesus, through the Immaculate Heart of Mary, I offer You my prayers, works, joys and sufferings of this day for all the intentions of Your Sacred Heart, in union with the Holy Sacrifice of the Mass throughout the world, in reparation for my sins, for the intentions of all my relatives and friends, and in particular for the intentions of the Holy Father. Amen.

READ & WRITE IT: BIBLE VERSE

REFLECT: WHAT DOES THIS MEAN TO ME?

RESPOND: WHAT DO I SAY TO GOD ABOUT THIS?

REST IN MEDITATION: HOW IS GOD ASKING ME TO CHANGE?

Lectio Devina

1. Ask God to see your day and actions through His eyes
2. Thank Him
3. Review and meditate on your day and actions
4. Face your shortcomings
5. Ask God for guidance and pray about tomorrow

I'M THANKFUL FOR...

MY SINS & SHORTCOMINGS TODAY

Examen

Day 9

O Jesus, through the Immaculate Heart of Mary, I offer You my prayers, works, joys and sufferings of this day for all the intentions of Your Sacred Heart, in union with the Holy Sacrifice of the Mass throughout the world, in reparation for my sins, for the intentions of all my relatives and friends, and in particular for the intentions of the Holy Father. Amen.

Lectio Devina

READ & WRITE IT OUT: BIBLE VERSE

REFLECT: WHAT DOES THIS MEAN TO ME?

RESPOND: WHAT DO I SAY TO GOD ABOUT THIS?

REST IN MEDITATION: HOW IS GOD ASKING ME TO CHANGE?

Examen

1. Ask God to see your day and actions through His eyes
2. Thank Him
3. Review and meditate on your day and actions
4. Face your shortcomings
5. Ask God for guidance and pray about tomorrow

I'M THANKFUL FOR...

MY SINS & SHORTCOMINGS TODAY

Day 10

Morning Prayer

O Jesus, through the Immaculate Heart of Mary, I offer You my prayers, works, joys and sufferings of this day for all the intentions of Your Sacred Heart, in union with the Holy Sacrifice of the Mass throughout the world, in reparation for my sins, for the intentions of all my relatives and friends, and in particular for the intentions of the Holy Father. Amen.

Lectio Devina

READ & WRITE IT: BIBLE VERSE

REFLECT: WHAT DOES THIS MEAN TO ME?

RESPOND: WHAT DO I SAY TO GOD ABOUT THIS?

REST IN MEDITATION: HOW IS GOD ASKING ME TO CHANGE?

Examen

1. Ask God to see your day and actions through His eyes
2. Thank Him
3. Review and meditate on your day and actions
4. Face your shortcomings
5. Ask God for guidance and pray about tomorrow

I'M THANKFUL FOR...

MY SINS & SHORTCOMINGS TODAY

Day 11

Morning Prayer

O Jesus, through the Immaculate Heart of Mary, I offer You my prayers, works, joys and sufferings of this day for all the intentions of Your Sacred Heart, in union with the Holy Sacrifice of the Mass throughout the world, in reparation for my sins, for the intentions of all my relatives and friends, and in particular for the intentions of the Holy Father. Amen.

Lectio Devina

READ & WRITE IT OUT: BIBLE VERSE

REFLECT: WHAT DOES THIS MEAN TO ME?

RESPOND: WHAT DO I SAY TO GOD ABOUT THIS?

REST IN MEDITATION: HOW IS GOD ASKING ME TO CHANGE?

Examen

1. Ask God to see your day and actions through His eyes
2. Thank Him
3. Review and meditate on your day and actions
4. Face your shortcomings
5. Ask God for guidance and pray about tomorrow

I'M THANKFUL FOR...

MY SINS & SHORTCOMINGS TODAY

Day 12

Morning Prayer

O Jesus, through the Immaculate Heart of Mary, I offer You my prayers, works, joys and sufferings of this day for all the intentions of Your Sacred Heart, in union with the Holy Sacrifice of the Mass throughout the world, in reparation for my sins, for the intentions of all my relatives and friends, and in particular for the intentions of the Holy Father. Amen.

Lectio Devina

READ & WRITE IT: BIBLE VERSE

REFLECT: WHAT DOES THIS MEAN TO ME?

RESPOND: WHAT DO I SAY TO GOD ABOUT THIS?

REST IN MEDITATION: HOW IS GOD ASKING ME TO CHANGE?

Examen

1. Ask God to see your day and actions through His eyes
2. Thank Him
3. Review and meditate on your day and actions
4. Face your shortcomings
5. Ask God for guidance and pray about tomorrow

I'M THANKFUL FOR...

MY SINS & SHORTCOMINGS TODAY

Day 13

O Jesus, through the Immaculate Heart of Mary, I offer You my prayers, works, joys and sufferings of this day for all the intentions of Your Sacred Heart, in union with the Holy Sacrifice of the Mass throughout the world, in reparation for my sins, for the intentions of all my relatives and friends, and in particular for the intentions of the Holy Father. Amen.

Lectio Devina

READ & WRITE IT OUT: BIBLE VERSE

REFLECT: WHAT DOES THIS MEAN TO ME?

RESPOND: WHAT DO I SAY TO GOD ABOUT THIS?

REST IN MEDITATION: HOW IS GOD ASKING ME TO CHANGE?

Examen

1. Ask God to see your day and actions through His eyes
2. Thank Him
3. Review and meditate on your day and actions
4. Face your shortcomings
5. Ask God for guidance and pray about tomorrow

I'M THANKFUL FOR...

MY SINS & SHORTCOMINGS TODAY

Day 14

Morning Prayer

O Jesus, through the Immaculate Heart of Mary, I offer You my prayers, works, joys and sufferings of this day for all the intentions of Your Sacred Heart, in union with the Holy Sacrifice of the Mass throughout the world, in reparation for my sins, for the intentions of all my relatives and friends, and in particular for the intentions of the Holy Father. Amen.

Lec-io Devina

READ & WRITE IT: BIBLE VERSE

REFLECT: WHAT DOES THIS MEAN TO ME?

RESPOND: WHAT DO I SAY TO GOD ABOUT THIS?

REST IN MEDITATION: HOW IS GOD ASKING ME TO CHANGE?

Examen

1. Ask God to see your day and actions through His eyes
2. Thank Him
3. Review and meditate on your day and actions
4. Face your shortcomings
5. Ask God for guidance and pray about tomorrow

I'M THANKFUL FOR...

MY SINS & SHORTCOMINGS TODAY

Day 15

Morning Prayer

Morning Prayer

O Jesus, through the Immaculate Heart of Mary, I offer You my prayers, works, joys and sufferings of this day for all the intentions of Your Sacred Heart, in union with the Holy Sacrifice of the Mass throughout the world, in reparation for my sins, for the intentions of all my relatives and friends, and in particular for the intentions of the Holy Father. Amen.

Lectio Devina

READ & WRITE IT OUT: BIBLE VERSE

REFLECT: WHAT DOES THIS MEAN TO ME?

RESPOND: WHAT DO I SAY TO GOD ABOUT THIS?

REST IN MEDITATION: HOW IS GOD ASKING ME TO CHANGE?

Examen

1. Ask God to see your day and actions through His eyes
2. Thank Him
3. Review and meditate on your day and actions
4. Face your shortcomings
5. Ask God for guidance and pray about tomorrow

I'M THANKFUL FOR...

MY SINS & SHORTCOMINGS TODAY

Day 16

Morning Prayer

O Jesus, through the Immaculate Heart of Mary, I offer You my prayers, works, joys and sufferings of this day for all the intentions of Your Sacred Heart, in union with the Holy Sacrifice of the Mass throughout the world, in reparation for my sins, for the intentions of all my relatives and friends, and in particular for the intentions of the Holy Father. Amen.

Lectio Devina

READ & WRITE IT: BIBLE VERSE

REFLECT: WHAT DOES THIS MEAN TO ME?

RESPOND: WHAT DO I SAY TO GOD ABOUT THIS?

REST IN MEDITATION: HOW IS GOD ASKING ME TO CHANGE?

Examen

1. Ask God to see your day and actions through His eyes
2. Thank Him
3. Review and meditate on your day and actions
4. Face your shortcomings
5. Ask God for guidance and pray about tomorrow

I'M THANKFUL FOR...

MY SINS & SHORTCOMINGS TODAY

Day 17   *Morning Prayer*

O Jesus, through the Immaculate Heart of Mary, I offer You my prayers, works, joys and sufferings of this day for all the intentions of Your Sacred Heart, in union with the Holy Sacrifice of the Mass throughout the world, in reparation for my sins, for the intentions of all my relatives and friends, and in particular for the intentions of the Holy Father. Amen.

READ & WRITE IT OUT: BIBLE VERSE

Lectio Devina

REFLECT: WHAT DOES THIS MEAN TO ME?

RESPOND: WHAT DO I SAY TO GOD ABOUT THIS?

REST IN MEDITATION: HOW IS GOD ASKING ME TO CHANGE?

Examen

1. Ask God to see your day and actions through His eyes
2. Thank Him
3. Review and meditate on your day and actions
4. Face your shortcomings
5. Ask God for guidance and pray about tomorrow

I'M THANKFUL FOR...   MY SINS & SHORTCOMINGS TODAY

Day 18   *Morning Prayer*

O Jesus, through the Immaculate Heart of Mary, I offer You my prayers, works, joys and sufferings of this day for all the intentions of Your Sacred Heart, in union with the Holy Sacrifice of the Mass throughout the world, in reparation for my sins, for the intentions of all my relatives and friends, and in particular for the intentions of the Holy Father. Amen.

READ & WRITE IT: BIBLE VERSE

Lectio Devina

REFLECT: WHAT DOES THIS MEAN TO ME?

RESPOND: WHAT DO I SAY TO GOD ABOUT THIS?

REST IN MEDITATION: HOW IS GOD ASKING ME TO CHANGE?

Examen

1. Ask God to see your day and actions through His eyes
2. Thank Him
3. Review and meditate on your day and actions
4. Face your shortcomings
5. Ask God for guidance and pray about tomorrow

I'M THANKFUL FOR...   MY SINS & SHORTCOMINGS TODAY

Day 19

O Jesus, through the Immaculate Heart of Mary, I offer You my prayers, works, joys and sufferings of this day for all the intentions of Your Sacred Heart, in union with the Holy Sacrifice of the Mass throughout the world, in reparation for my sins, for the intentions of all my relatives and friends, and in particular for the intentions of the Holy Father. Amen.

Lectio Devina

READ & WRITE IT OUT: BIBLE VERSE

REFLECT: WHAT DOES THIS MEAN TO ME?

RESPOND: WHAT DO I SAY TO GOD ABOUT THIS?

REST IN MEDITATION: HOW IS GOD ASKING ME TO CHANGE?

Examen

1. Ask God to see your day and actions through His eyes
2. Thank Him
3. Review and meditate on your day and actions
4. Face your shortcomings
5. Ask God for guidance and pray about tomorrow

I'M THANKFUL FOR...

MY SINS & SHORTCOMINGS TODAY

Day 20

Morning Prayer

O Jesus, through the Immaculate Heart of Mary, I offer You my prayers, works, joys and sufferings of this day for all the intentions of Your Sacred Heart, in union with the Holy Sacrifice of the Mass throughout the world, in reparation for my sins, for the intentions of all my relatives and friends, and in particular for the intentions of the Holy Father. Amen.

Lectio Devina

READ & WRITE IT: BIBLE VERSE

REFLECT: WHAT DOES THIS MEAN TO ME?

RESPOND: WHAT DO I SAY TO GOD ABOUT THIS?

REST IN MEDITATION: HOW IS GOD ASKING ME TO CHANGE?

Examen

1. Ask God to see your day and actions through His eyes
2. Thank Him
3. Review and meditate on your day and actions
4. Face your shortcomings
5. Ask God for guidance and pray about tomorrow

I'M THANKFUL FOR...

MY SINS & SHORTCOMINGS TODAY

Day 21

O Jesus, through the Immaculate Heart of Mary, I offer You my prayers, works, joys and sufferings of this day for all the intentions of Your Sacred Heart, in union with the Holy Sacrifice of the Mass throughout the world, in reparation for my sins, for the intentions of all my relatives and friends, and in particular for the intentions of the Holy Father. Amen.

Lectio Devina

READ & WRITE IT OUT: BIBLE VERSE

REFLECT: WHAT DOES THIS MEAN TO ME?

RESPOND: WHAT DO I SAY TO GOD ABOUT THIS?

REST IN MEDITATION: HOW IS GOD ASKING ME TO CHANGE?

Examen

1. Ask God to see your day and actions through His eyes
2. Thank Him
3. Review and meditate on your day and actions
4. Face your shortcomings
5. Ask God for guidance and pray about tomorrow

I'M THANKFUL FOR...

MY SINS & SHORTCOMINGS TODAY

Day 22

Morning Prayer

O Jesus, through the Immaculate Heart of Mary, I offer You my prayers, works, joys and sufferings of this day for all the intentions of Your Sacred Heart, in union with the Holy Sacrifice of the Mass throughout the world, in reparation for my sins, for the intentions of all my relatives and friends, and in particular for the intentions of the Holy Father. Amen.

Lectio Devina

READ & WRITE IT: BIBLE VERSE

REFLECT: WHAT DOES THIS MEAN TO ME?

RESPOND: WHAT DO I SAY TO GOD ABOUT THIS?

REST IN MEDITATION: HOW IS GOD ASKING ME TO CHANGE?

Examen

1. Ask God to see your day and actions through His eyes
2. Thank Him
3. Review and meditate on your day and actions
4. Face your shortcomings
5. Ask God for guidance and pray about tomorrow

I'M THANKFUL FOR...

MY SINS & SHORTCOMINGS TODAY

Day 23

Morning Prayer

O Jesus, through the Immaculate Heart of Mary, I offer You my prayers, works, joys and sufferings of this day for all the intentions of Your Sacred Heart, in union with the Holy Sacrifice of the Mass throughout the world, in reparation for my sins, for the intentions of all my relatives and friends, and in particular for the intentions of the Holy Father. Amen.

READ & WRITE IT OUT: BIBLE VERSE

REFLECT: WHAT DOES THIS MEAN TO ME?

RESPOND: WHAT DO I SAY TO GOD ABOUT THIS?

REST IN MEDITATION: HOW IS GOD ASKING ME TO CHANGE?

Lectio Devina

1. Ask God to see your day and actions through His eyes
2. Thank Him
3. Review and meditate on your day and actions
4. Face your shortcomings
5. Ask God for guidance and pray about tomorrow

I'M THANKFUL FOR...

MY SINS & SHORTCOMINGS TODAY

Examen

Day 24

Morning Prayer

O Jesus, through the Immaculate Heart of Mary, I offer You my prayers, works, joys and sufferings of this day for all the intentions of Your Sacred Heart, in union with the Holy Sacrifice of the Mass throughout the world, in reparation for my sins, for the intentions of all my relatives and friends, and in particular for the intentions of the Holy Father. Amen.

READ & WRITE IT: BIBLE VERSE

REFLECT: WHAT DOES THIS MEAN TO ME?

RESPOND: WHAT DO I SAY TO GOD ABOUT THIS?

REST IN MEDITATION: HOW IS GOD ASKING ME TO CHANGE?

Lectio Devina

1. Ask God to see your day and actions through His eyes
2. Thank Him
3. Review and meditate on your day and actions
4. Face your shortcomings
5. Ask God for guidance and pray about tomorrow

I'M THANKFUL FOR...

MY SINS & SHORTCOMINGS TODAY

Examen

Day 25

Morning Prayer

Morning Prayer

O Jesus, through the Immaculate Heart of Mary, I offer You my prayers, works, joys and sufferings of this day for all the intentions of Your Sacred Heart, in union with the Holy Sacrifice of the Mass throughout the world, in reparation for my sins, for the intentions of all my relatives and friends, and in particular for the intentions of the Holy Father. Amen.

Lectio Devina

READ & WRITE IT OUT: BIBLE VERSE

REFLECT: WHAT DOES THIS MEAN TO ME?

RESPOND: WHAT DO I SAY TO GOD ABOUT THIS?

REST IN MEDITATION: HOW IS GOD ASKING ME TO CHANGE?

Examen

1. Ask God to see your day and actions through His eyes
2. Thank Him
3. Review and meditate on your day and actions
4. Face your shortcomings
5. Ask God for guidance and pray about tomorrow

I'M THANKFUL FOR...

MY SINS & SHORTCOMINGS TODAY

Day 26

Morning Prayer

O Jesus, through the Immaculate Heart of Mary, I offer You my prayers, works, joys and sufferings of this day for all the intentions of Your Sacred Heart, in union with the Holy Sacrifice of the Mass throughout the world, in reparation for my sins, for the intentions of all my relatives and friends, and in particular for the intentions of the Holy Father. Amen.

Lectio Devina

READ & WRITE IT: BIBLE VERSE

REFLECT: WHAT DOES THIS MEAN TO ME?

RESPOND: WHAT DO I SAY TO GOD ABOUT THIS?

REST IN MEDITATION: HOW IS GOD ASKING ME TO CHANGE?

Examen

1. Ask God to see your day and actions through His eyes
2. Thank Him
3. Review and meditate on your day and actions
4. Face your shortcomings
5. Ask God for guidance and pray about tomorrow

I'M THANKFUL FOR...

MY SINS & SHORTCOMINGS TODAY

Day 27

O Jesus, through the Immaculate Heart of Mary, I offer You my prayers, works, joys and sufferings of this day for all the intentions of Your Sacred Heart, in union with the Holy Sacrifice of the Mass throughout the world, in reparation for my sins, for the intentions of all my relatives and friends, and in particular for the intentions of the Holy Father. Amen.

Lectio Devina

READ & WRITE IT OUT: BIBLE VERSE

REFLECT: WHAT DOES THIS MEAN TO ME?

RESPOND: WHAT DO I SAY TO GOD ABOUT THIS?

REST IN MEDITATION: HOW IS GOD ASKING ME TO CHANGE?

Examen

1. Ask God to see your day and actions through His eyes
2. Thank Him
3. Review and meditate on your day and actions
4. Face your shortcomings
5. Ask God for guidance and pray about tomorrow

I'M THANKFUL FOR...

MY SINS & SHORTCOMINGS TODAY

Day 28

Morning Prayer

O Jesus, through the Immaculate Heart of Mary, I offer You my prayers, works, joys and sufferings of this day for all the intentions of Your Sacred Heart, in union with the Holy Sacrifice of the Mass throughout the world, in reparation for my sins, for the intentions of all my relatives and friends, and in particular for the intentions of the Holy Father. Amen.

Lectio Devina

READ & WRITE IT: BIBLE VERSE

REFLECT: WHAT DOES THIS MEAN TO ME?

RESPOND: WHAT DO I SAY TO GOD ABOUT THIS?

REST IN MEDITATION: HOW IS GOD ASKING ME TO CHANGE?

Examen

1. Ask God to see your day and actions through His eyes
2. Thank Him
3. Review and meditate on your day and actions
4. Face your shortcomings
5. Ask God for guidance and pray about tomorrow

I'M THANKFUL FOR...

MY SINS & SHORTCOMINGS TODAY

Day 29

O Jesus, through the Immaculate Heart of Mary, I offer You my prayers, works, joys and sufferings of this day for all the intentions of Your Sacred Heart, in union with the Holy Sacrifice of the Mass throughout the world, in reparation for my sins, for the intentions of all my relatives and friends, and in particular for the intentions of the Holy Father. Amen.

Lectio Devina

READ & WRITE IT OUT: BIBLE VERSE

REFLECT: WHAT DOES THIS MEAN TO ME?

RESPOND: WHAT DO I SAY TO GOD ABOUT THIS?

REST IN MEDITATION: HOW IS GOD ASKING ME TO CHANGE?

Examen

1. Ask God to see your day and actions through His eyes
2. Thank Him
3. Review and meditate on your day and actions
4. Face your shortcomings
5. Ask God for guidance and pray about tomorrow

I'M THANKFUL FOR...

MY SINS & SHORTCOMINGS TODAY

Day 30

Morning Prayer

O Jesus, through the Immaculate Heart of Mary, I offer You my prayers, works, joys and sufferings of this day for all the intentions of Your Sacred Heart, in union with the Holy Sacrifice of the Mass throughout the world, in reparation for my sins, for the intentions of all my relatives and friends, and in particular for the intentions of the Holy Father. Amen.

Lectio Devina

READ & WRITE IT: BIBLE VERSE

REFLECT: WHAT DOES THIS MEAN TO ME?

RESPOND: WHAT DO I SAY TO GOD ABOUT THIS?

REST IN MEDITATION: HOW IS GOD ASKING ME TO CHANGE?

Examen

1. Ask God to see your day and actions through His eyes
2. Thank Him
3. Review and meditate on your day and actions
4. Face your shortcomings
5. Ask God for guidance and pray about tomorrow

I'M THANKFUL FOR...

MY SINS & SHORTCOMINGS TODAY

Day 31

O Jesus, through the Immaculate Heart of Mary, I offer You my prayers, works, joys and sufferings of this day for all the intentions of Your Sacred Heart, in union with the Holy Sacrifice of the Mass throughout the world, in reparation for my sins, for the intentions of all my relatives and friends, and in particular for the intentions of the Holy Father. Amen.

Lectio Devina

READ & WRITE IT OUT: BIBLE VERSE

REFLECT: WHAT DOES THIS MEAN TO ME?

RESPOND: WHAT DO I SAY TO GOD ABOUT THIS?

REST IN MEDITATION: HOW IS GOD ASKING ME TO CHANGE?

Examen

1. Ask God to see your day and actions through His eyes
2. Thank Him
3. Review and meditate on your day and actions
4. Face your shortcomings
5. Ask God for guidance and pray about tomorrow

I'M THANKFUL FOR...

MY SINS & SHORTCOMINGS TODAY

PRAYERS & REFLECTIONS ON YOUR SPIRITUAL JOURNEY THIS MONTH

April

"Be who you were created to be, and you will set the world on fire."
-St. Catherine of Siena

PERSONAL RESOLUTIONS

SPIRITUAL READING LOG

LAST CONFESSION DATE

HOLY ACTIVITIES WITH MY FAMILY/ FRIENDS

PRAYER REQUESTS

✔ ROSARY & CHAPLET TRACKER

"We are all called to be great saints; don't miss the opportunity!" - Mother Angelica

Day 1

Morning Prayer

O Jesus, through the Immaculate Heart of Mary, I offer You my prayers, works, joys and sufferings of this day for all the intentions of Your Sacred Heart, in union with the Holy Sacrifice of the Mass throughout the world, in reparation for my sins, for the intentions of all my relatives and friends, and in particular for the intentions of the Holy Father. Amen.

Lectio Devina

READ & WRITE IT OUT: BIBLE VERSE

REFLECT: WHAT DOES THIS MEAN TO ME?

RESPOND: WHAT DO I SAY TO GOD ABOUT THIS?

REST IN MEDITATION: HOW IS GOD ASKING ME TO CHANGE?

Examen

1. Ask God to see your day and actions through His eyes
2. Thank Him
3. Review and meditate on your day and actions
4. Face your shortcomings
5. Ask God for guidance and pray about tomorrow

I'M THANKFUL FOR...

MY SINS & SHORTCOMINGS TODAY

Day 2

Morning Prayer

O Jesus, through the Immaculate Heart of Mary, I offer You my prayers, works, joys and sufferings of this day for all the intentions of Your Sacred Heart, in union with the Holy Sacrifice of the Mass throughout the world, in reparation for my sins, for the intentions of all my relatives and friends, and in particular for the intentions of the Holy Father. Amen.

Lectio Devina

READ & WRITE IT: BIBLE VERSE

REFLECT: WHAT DOES THIS MEAN TO ME?

RESPOND: WHAT DO I SAY TO GOD ABOUT THIS?

REST IN MEDITATION: HOW IS GOD ASKING ME TO CHANGE?

Examen

1. Ask God to see your day and actions through His eyes
2. Thank Him
3. Review and meditate on your day and actions
4. Face your shortcomings
5. Ask God for guidance and pray about tomorrow

I'M THANKFUL FOR...

MY SINS & SHORTCOMINGS TODAY

Day 3   *Morning Prayer*

O Jesus, through the Immaculate Heart of Mary, I offer You my prayers, works, joys and sufferings of this day for all the intentions of Your Sacred Heart, in union with the Holy Sacrifice of the Mass throughout the world, in reparation for my sins, for the intentions of all my relatives and friends, and in particular for the intentions of the Holy Father. Amen.

Lectio Devina

READ & WRITE IT OUT: BIBLE VERSE

REFLECT: WHAT DOES THIS MEAN TO ME?

RESPOND: WHAT DO I SAY TO GOD ABOUT THIS?

REST IN MEDITATION: HOW IS GOD ASKING ME TO CHANGE?

Examen

1. Ask God to see your day and actions through His eyes
2. Thank Him
3. Review and meditate on your day and actions
4. Face your shortcomings
5. Ask God for guidance and pray about tomorrow

I'M THANKFUL FOR...   MY SINS & SHORTCOMINGS TODAY

Day 4   *Morning Prayer*

O Jesus, through the Immaculate Heart of Mary, I offer You my prayers, works, joys and sufferings of this day for all the intentions of Your Sacred Heart, in union with the Holy Sacrifice of the Mass throughout the world, in reparation for my sins, for the intentions of all my relatives and friends, and in particular for the intentions of the Holy Father. Amen.

Lectio Devina

READ & WRITE IT: BIBLE VERSE

REFLECT: WHAT DOES THIS MEAN TO ME?

RESPOND: WHAT DO I SAY TO GOD ABOUT THIS?

REST IN MEDITATION: HOW IS GOD ASKING ME TO CHANGE?

Examen

1. Ask God to see your day and actions through His eyes
2. Thank Him
3. Review and meditate on your day and actions
4. Face your shortcomings
5. Ask God for guidance and pray about tomorrow

I'M THANKFUL FOR...   MY SINS & SHORTCOMINGS TODAY

Day 5

Morning Prayer

O Jesus, through the Immaculate Heart of Mary, I offer You my prayers, works, joys and sufferings of this day for all the intentions of Your Sacred Heart, in union with the Holy Sacrifice of the Mass throughout the world, in reparation for my sins, for the intentions of all my relatives and friends, and in particular for the intentions of the Holy Father. Amen.

Lectio Devina

READ & WRITE IT OUT: BIBLE VERSE

REFLECT: WHAT DOES THIS MEAN TO ME?

RESPOND: WHAT DO I SAY TO GOD ABOUT THIS?

REST IN MEDITATION: HOW IS GOD ASKING ME TO CHANGE?

Examen

1. Ask God to see your day and actions through His eyes
2. Thank Him
3. Review and meditate on your day and actions
4. Face your shortcomings
5. Ask God for guidance and pray about tomorrow

I'M THANKFUL FOR...

MY SINS & SHORTCOMINGS TODAY

Day 6

Morning Prayer

O Jesus, through the Immaculate Heart of Mary, I offer You my prayers, works, joys and sufferings of this day for all the intentions of Your Sacred Heart, in union with the Holy Sacrifice of the Mass throughout the world, in reparation for my sins, for the intentions of all my relatives and friends, and in particular for the intentions of the Holy Father. Amen.

Lectio Devina

READ & WRITE IT: BIBLE VERSE

REFLECT: WHAT DOES THIS MEAN TO ME?

RESPOND: WHAT DO I SAY TO GOD ABOUT THIS?

REST IN MEDITATION: HOW IS GOD ASKING ME TO CHANGE?

Examen

1. Ask God to see your day and actions through His eyes
2. Thank Him
3. Review and meditate on your day and actions
4. Face your shortcomings
5. Ask God for guidance and pray about tomorrow

I'M THANKFUL FOR...

MY SINS & SHORTCOMINGS TODAY

Day 7

Morning Prayer

O Jesus, through the Immaculate Heart of Mary, I offer You my prayers, works, joys and sufferings of this day for all the intentions of Your Sacred Heart, in union with the Holy Sacrifice of the Mass throughout the world, in reparation for my sins, for the intentions of all my relatives and friends, and in particular for the intentions of the Holy Father. Amen.

Lectio Devina

READ & WRITE IT OUT: BIBLE VERSE

REFLECT: WHAT DOES THIS MEAN TO ME?

RESPOND: WHAT DO I SAY TO GOD ABOUT THIS?

REST IN MEDITATION: HOW IS GOD ASKING ME TO CHANGE?

Examen

1. Ask God to see your day and actions through His eyes
2. Thank Him
3. Review and meditate on your day and actions
4. Face your shortcomings
5. Ask God for guidance and pray about tomorrow

I'M THANKFUL FOR...

MY SINS & SHORTCOMINGS TODAY

Day 8

Morning Prayer

O Jesus, through the Immaculate Heart of Mary, I offer You my prayers, works, joys and sufferings of this day for all the intentions of Your Sacred Heart, in union with the Holy Sacrifice of the Mass throughout the world, in reparation for my sins, for the intentions of all my relatives and friends, and in particular for the intentions of the Holy Father. Amen.

Lectio Devina

READ & WRITE IT: BIBLE VERSE

REFLECT: WHAT DOES THIS MEAN TO ME?

RESPOND: WHAT DO I SAY TO GOD ABOUT THIS?

REST IN MEDITATION: HOW IS GOD ASKING ME TO CHANGE?

Examen

1. Ask God to see your day and actions through His eyes
2. Thank Him
3. Review and meditate on your day and actions
4. Face your shortcomings
5. Ask God for guidance and pray about tomorrow

I'M THANKFUL FOR...

MY SINS & SHORTCOMINGS TODAY

Day 9

O Jesus, through the Immaculate Heart of Mary, I offer You my prayers, works, joys and sufferings of this day for all the intentions of Your Sacred Heart, in union with the Holy Sacrifice of the Mass throughout the world, in reparation for my sins, for the intentions of all my relatives and friends, and in particular for the intentions of the Holy Father. Amen.

Lectio Devina

READ & WRITE IT OUT: BIBLE VERSE

REFLECT: WHAT DOES THIS MEAN TO ME?

RESPOND: WHAT DO I SAY TO GOD ABOUT THIS?

REST IN MEDITATION: HOW IS GOD ASKING ME TO CHANGE?

Examen

1. Ask God to see your day and actions through His eyes
2. Thank Him
3. Review and meditate on your day and actions
4. Face your shortcomings
5. Ask God for guidance and pray about tomorrow

I'M THANKFUL FOR...

MY SINS & SHORTCOMINGS TODAY

Day 10

Morning Prayer

O Jesus, through the Immaculate Heart of Mary, I offer You my prayers, works, joys and sufferings of this day for all the intentions of Your Sacred Heart, in union with the Holy Sacrifice of the Mass throughout the world, in reparation for my sins, for the intentions of all my relatives and friends, and in particular for the intentions of the Holy Father. Amen.

Lectio Devina

READ & WRITE IT: BIBLE VERSE

REFLECT: WHAT DOES THIS MEAN TO ME?

RESPOND: WHAT DO I SAY TO GOD ABOUT THIS?

REST IN MEDITATION: HOW IS GOD ASKING ME TO CHANGE?

Examen

1. Ask God to see your day and actions through His eyes
2. Thank Him
3. Review and meditate on your day and actions
4. Face your shortcomings
5. Ask God for guidance and pray about tomorrow

I'M THANKFUL FOR...

MY SINS & SHORTCOMINGS TODAY

Day 11

Morning Prayer

O Jesus, through the Immaculate Heart of Mary, I offer You my prayers, works, joys and sufferings of this day for all the intentions of Your Sacred Heart, in union with the Holy Sacrifice of the Mass throughout the world, in reparation for my sins, for the intentions of all my relatives and friends, and in particular for the intentions of the Holy Father. Amen.

Lectio Devina

READ & WRITE IT OUT: BIBLE VERSE

REFLECT: WHAT DOES THIS MEAN TO ME?

RESPOND: WHAT DO I SAY TO GOD ABOUT THIS?

REST IN MEDITATION: HOW IS GOD ASKING ME TO CHANGE?

Examen

1. Ask God to see your day and actions through His eyes
2. Thank Him
3. Review and meditate on your day and actions
4. Face your shortcomings
5. Ask God for guidance and pray about tomorrow

I'M THANKFUL FOR...

MY SINS & SHORTCOMINGS TODAY

Day 12

Morning Prayer

O Jesus, through the Immaculate Heart of Mary, I offer You my prayers, works, joys and sufferings of this day for all the intentions of Your Sacred Heart, in union with the Holy Sacrifice of the Mass throughout the world, in reparation for my sins, for the intentions of all my relatives and friends, and in particular for the intentions of the Holy Father. Amen.

Lectio Devina

READ & WRITE IT: BIBLE VERSE

REFLECT: WHAT DOES THIS MEAN TO ME?

RESPOND: WHAT DO I SAY TO GOD ABOUT THIS?

REST IN MEDITATION: HOW IS GOD ASKING ME TO CHANGE?

Examen

1. Ask God to see your day and actions through His eyes
2. Thank Him
3. Review and meditate on your day and actions
4. Face your shortcomings
5. Ask God for guidance and pray about tomorrow

I'M THANKFUL FOR...

MY SINS & SHORTCOMINGS TODAY

Day 13

O Jesus, through the Immaculate Heart of Mary, I offer You my prayers, works, joys and sufferings of this day for all the intentions of Your Sacred Heart, in union with the Holy Sacrifice of the Mass throughout the world, in reparation for my sins, for the intentions of all my relatives and friends, and in particular for the intentions of the Holy Father. Amen.

Lectio Devina

READ & WRITE IT OUT: BIBLE VERSE

REFLECT: WHAT DOES THIS MEAN TO ME?

RESPOND: WHAT DO I SAY TO GOD ABOUT THIS?

REST IN MEDITATION: HOW IS GOD ASKING ME TO CHANGE?

Examen

1. Ask God to see your day and actions through His eyes
2. Thank Him
3. Review and meditate on your day and actions
4. Face your shortcomings
5. Ask God for guidance and pray about tomorrow

I'M THANKFUL FOR...

MY SINS & SHORTCOMINGS TODAY

Day 14

Morning Prayer

O Jesus, through the Immaculate Heart of Mary, I offer You my prayers, works, joys and sufferings of this day for all the intentions of Your Sacred Heart, in union with the Holy Sacrifice of the Mass throughout the world, in reparation for my sins, for the intentions of all my relatives and friends, and in particular for the intentions of the Holy Father. Amen.

Lectio Devina

READ & WRITE IT: BIBLE VERSE

REFLECT: WHAT DOES THIS MEAN TO ME?

RESPOND: WHAT DO I SAY TO GOD ABOUT THIS?

REST IN MEDITATION: HOW IS GOD ASKING ME TO CHANGE?

Examen

1. Ask God to see your day and actions through His eyes
2. Thank Him
3. Review and meditate on your day and actions
4. Face your shortcomings
5. Ask God for guidance and pray about tomorrow

I'M THANKFUL FOR...

MY SINS & SHORTCOMINGS TODAY

Day 15   *Morning Prayer*

O Jesus, through the Immaculate Heart of Mary, I offer You my prayers, works, joys and sufferings of this day for all the intentions of Your Sacred Heart, in union with the Holy Sacrifice of the Mass throughout the world, in reparation for my sins, for the intentions of all my relatives and friends, and in particular for the intentions of the Holy Father. Amen.

READ & WRITE IT OUT: BIBLE VERSE

REFLECT: WHAT DOES THIS MEAN TO ME?

RESPOND: WHAT DO I SAY TO GOD ABOUT THIS?

REST IN MEDITATION: HOW IS GOD ASKING ME TO CHANGE?

Lectio Devina

1. Ask God to see your day and actions through His eyes
2. Thank Him
3. Review and meditate on your day and actions
4. Face your shortcomings
5. Ask God for guidance and pray about tomorrow

I'M THANKFUL FOR...   MY SINS & SHORTCOMINGS TODAY

Examen

Day 16   *Morning Prayer*

O Jesus, through the Immaculate Heart of Mary, I offer You my prayers, works, joys and sufferings of this day for all the intentions of Your Sacred Heart, in union with the Holy Sacrifice of the Mass throughout the world, in reparation for my sins, for the intentions of all my relatives and friends, and in particular for the intentions of the Holy Father. Amen.

READ & WRITE IT: BIBLE VERSE

REFLECT: WHAT DOES THIS MEAN TO ME?

RESPOND: WHAT DO I SAY TO GOD ABOUT THIS?

REST IN MEDITATION: HOW IS GOD ASKING ME TO CHANGE?

Lect o Devina

1. Ask God to see your day and actions through His eyes
2. Thank Him
3. Review and meditate on your day and actions
4. Face your shortcomings
5. Ask God for guidance and pray about tomorrow

I'M THANKFUL FOR...   MY SINS & SHORTCOMINGS TODAY

Examen

Day 17

O Jesus, through the Immaculate Heart of Mary, I offer You my prayers, works, joys and sufferings of this day for all the intentions of Your Sacred Heart, in union with the Holy Sacrifice of the Mass throughout the world, in reparation for my sins, for the intentions of all my relatives and friends, and in particular for the intentions of the Holy Father. Amen.

Lectio Devina

READ & WRITE IT OUT: BIBLE VERSE

REFLECT: WHAT DOES THIS MEAN TO ME?

RESPOND: WHAT DO I SAY TO GOD ABOUT THIS?

REST IN MEDITATION: HOW IS GOD ASKING ME TO CHANGE?

Examen

1. Ask God to see your day and actions through His eyes
2. Thank Him
3. Review and meditate on your day and actions
4. Face your shortcomings
5. Ask God for guidance and pray about tomorrow

I'M THANKFUL FOR...

MY SINS & SHORTCOMINGS TODAY

Day 18

Morning Prayer

O Jesus, through the Immaculate Heart of Mary, I offer You my prayers, works, joys and sufferings of this day for all the intentions of Your Sacred Heart, in union with the Holy Sacrifice of the Mass throughout the world, in reparation for my sins, for the intentions of all my relatives and friends, and in particular for the intentions of the Holy Father. Amen.

Lectio Devina

READ & WRITE IT: BIBLE VERSE

REFLECT: WHAT DOES THIS MEAN TO ME?

RESPOND: WHAT DO I SAY TO GOD ABOUT THIS?

REST IN MEDITATION: HOW IS GOD ASKING ME TO CHANGE?

Examen

1. Ask God to see your day and actions through His eyes
2. Thank Him
3. Review and meditate on your day and actions
4. Face your shortcomings
5. Ask God for guidance and pray about tomorrow

I'M THANKFUL FOR...

MY SINS & SHORTCOMINGS TODAY

Day 19

O Jesus, through the Immaculate Heart of Mary, I offer You my prayers, works, joys and sufferings of this day for all the intentions of Your Sacred Heart, in union with the Holy Sacrifice of the Mass throughout the world, in reparation for my sins, for the intentions of all my relatives and friends, and in particular for the intentions of the Holy Father. Amen.

Lectio Devina

READ & WRITE IT OUT: BIBLE VERSE

REFLECT: WHAT DOES THIS MEAN TO ME?

RESPOND: WHAT DO I SAY TO GOD ABOUT THIS?

REST IN MEDITATION: HOW IS GOD ASKING ME TO CHANGE?

Examen

1. Ask God to see your day and actions through His eyes
2. Thank Him
3. Review and meditate on your day and actions
4. Face your shortcomings
5. Ask God for guidance and pray about tomorrow

I'M THANKFUL FOR...

MY SINS & SHORTCOMINGS TODAY

Day 20

Morning Prayer

O Jesus, through the Immaculate Heart of Mary, I offer You my prayers, works, joys and sufferings of this day for all the intentions of Your Sacred Heart, in union with the Holy Sacrifice of the Mass throughout the world, in reparation for my sins, for the intentions of all my relatives and friends, and in particular for the intentions of the Holy Father. Amen.

Lectio Devina

READ & WRITE IT: BIBLE VERSE

REFLECT: WHAT DOES THIS MEAN TO ME?

RESPOND: WHAT DO I SAY TO GOD ABOUT THIS?

REST IN MEDITATION: HOW IS GOD ASKING ME TO CHANGE?

Examen

1. Ask God to see your day and actions through His eyes
2. Thank Him
3. Review and meditate on your day and actions
4. Face your shortcomings
5. Ask God for guidance and pray about tomorrow

I'M THANKFUL FOR...

MY SINS & SHORTCOMINGS TODAY

Day 21

O Jesus, through the Immaculate Heart of Mary, I offer You my prayers, works, joys and sufferings of this day for all the intentions of Your Sacred Heart, in union with the Holy Sacrifice of the Mass throughout the world, in reparation for my sins, for the intentions of all my relatives and friends, and in particular for the intentions of the Holy Father. Amen.

Lectio Devina

READ & WRITE IT OUT: BIBLE VERSE

REFLECT: WHAT DOES THIS MEAN TO ME?

RESPOND: WHAT DO I SAY TO GOD ABOUT THIS?

REST IN MEDITATION: HOW IS GOD ASKING ME TO CHANGE?

Examen

1. Ask God to see your day and actions through His eyes
2. Thank Him
3. Review and meditate on your day and actions
4. Face your shortcomings
5. Ask God for guidance and pray about tomorrow

I'M THANKFUL FOR...

MY SINS & SHORTCOMINGS TODAY

Day 22

Morning Prayer

O Jesus, through the Immaculate Heart of Mary, I offer You my prayers, works, joys and sufferings of this day for all the intentions of Your Sacred Heart, in union with the Holy Sacrifice of the Mass throughout the world, in reparation for my sins, for the intentions of all my relatives and friends, and in particular for the intentions of the Holy Father. Amen.

Lectio Devina

READ & WRITE IT: BIBLE VERSE

REFLECT: WHAT DOES THIS MEAN TO ME?

RESPOND: WHAT DO I SAY TO GOD ABOUT THIS?

REST IN MEDITATION: HOW IS GOD ASKING ME TO CHANGE?

Examen

1. Ask God to see your day and actions through His eyes
2. Thank Him
3. Review and meditate on your day and actions
4. Face your shortcomings
5. Ask God for guidance and pray about tomorrow

I'M THANKFUL FOR...

MY SINS & SHORTCOMINGS TODAY

Day 23

O Jesus, through the Immaculate Heart of Mary, I offer You my prayers, works, joys and sufferings of this day for all the intentions of Your Sacred Heart, in union with the Holy Sacrifice of the Mass throughout the world, in reparation for my sins, for the intentions of all my relatives and friends, and in particular for the intentions of the Holy Father. Amen.

Lectio Devina

READ & WRITE IT OUT: BIBLE VERSE

REFLECT: WHAT DOES THIS MEAN TO ME?

RESPOND: WHAT DO I SAY TO GOD ABOUT THIS?

REST IN MEDITATION: HOW IS GOD ASKING ME TO CHANGE?

Examen

1. Ask God to see your day and actions through His eyes
2. Thank Him
3. Review and meditate on your day and actions
4. Face your shortcomings
5. Ask God for guidance and pray about tomorrow

I'M THANKFUL FOR...

MY SINS & SHORTCOMINGS TODAY

Day 24

Morning Prayer

O Jesus, through the Immaculate Heart of Mary, I offer You my prayers, works, joys and sufferings of this day for all the intentions of Your Sacred Heart, in union with the Holy Sacrifice of the Mass throughout the world, in reparation for my sins, for the intentions of all my relatives and friends, and in particular for the intentions of the Holy Father. Amen.

Lectio Devina

READ & WRITE IT: BIBLE VERSE

REFLECT: WHAT DOES THIS MEAN TO ME?

RESPOND: WHAT DO I SAY TO GOD ABOUT THIS?

REST IN MEDITATION: HOW IS GOD ASKING ME TO CHANGE?

Examen

1. Ask God to see your day and actions through His eyes
2. Thank Him
3. Review and meditate on your day and actions
4. Face your shortcomings
5. Ask God for guidance and pray about tomorrow

I'M THANKFUL FOR...

MY SINS & SHORTCOMINGS TODAY

Day 25   *Morning Prayer*

O Jesus, through the Immaculate Heart of Mary, I offer You my prayers, works, joys and sufferings of this day for all the intentions of Your Sacred Heart, in union with the Holy Sacrifice of the Mass throughout the world, in reparation for my sins, for the intentions of all my relatives and friends, and in particular for the intentions of the Holy Father. Amen.

Lectio Devina

READ & WRITE IT OUT: BIBLE VERSE

REFLECT: WHAT DOES THIS MEAN TO ME?

RESPOND: WHAT DO I SAY TO GOD ABOUT THIS?

REST IN MEDITATION: HOW IS GOD ASKING ME TO CHANGE?

Examen

1. Ask God to see your day and actions through His eyes
2. Thank Him
3. Review and meditate on your day and actions
4. Face your shortcomings
5. Ask God for guidance and pray about tomorrow

I'M THANKFUL FOR...

MY SINS & SHORTCOMINGS TODAY

Day 26   *Morning Prayer*

O Jesus, through the Immaculate Heart of Mary, I offer You my prayers, works, joys and sufferings of this day for all the intentions of Your Sacred Heart, in union with the Holy Sacrifice of the Mass throughout the world, in reparation for my sins, for the intentions of all my relatives and friends, and in particular for the intentions of the Holy Father. Amen.

Lectio Devina

READ & WRITE IT: BIBLE VERSE

REFLECT: WHAT DOES THIS MEAN TO ME?

RESPOND: WHAT DO I SAY TO GOD ABOUT THIS?

REST IN MEDITATION: HOW IS GOD ASKING ME TO CHANGE?

Examen

1. Ask God to see your day and actions through His eyes
2. Thank Him
3. Review and meditate on your day and actions
4. Face your shortcomings
5. Ask God for guidance and pray about tomorrow

I'M THANKFUL FOR...

MY SINS & SHORTCOMINGS TODAY

Day 27   *Morning Prayer*

O Jesus, through the Immaculate Heart of Mary, I offer You my prayers, works, joys and sufferings of this day for all the intentions of Your Sacred Heart, in union with the Holy Sacrifice of the Mass throughout the world, in reparation for my sins, for the intentions of all my relatives and friends, and in particular for the intentions of the Holy Father. Amen.

Lectio Devina

READ & WRITE IT OUT: BIBLE VERSE

REFLECT: WHAT DOES THIS MEAN TO ME?

RESPOND: WHAT DO I SAY TO GOD ABOUT THIS?

REST IN MEDITATION: HOW IS GOD ASKING ME TO CHANGE?

Examen

1. Ask God to see your day and actions through His eyes
2. Thank Him
3. Review and meditate on your day and actions
4. Face your shortcomings
5. Ask God for guidance and pray about tomorrow

I'M THANKFUL FOR...

MY SINS & SHORTCOMINGS TODAY

Day 28   *Morning Prayer*

O Jesus, through the Immaculate Heart of Mary, I offer You my prayers, works, joys and sufferings of this day for all the intentions of Your Sacred Heart, in union with the Holy Sacrifice of the Mass throughout the world, in reparation for my sins, for the intentions of all my relatives and friends, and in particular for the intentions of the Holy Father. Amen.

Lectio Devina

READ & WRITE IT: BIBLE VERSE

REFLECT: WHAT DOES THIS MEAN TO ME?

RESPOND: WHAT DO I SAY TO GOD ABOUT THIS?

REST IN MEDITATION: HOW IS GOD ASKING ME TO CHANGE?

Examen

1. Ask God to see your day and actions through His eyes
2. Thank Him
3. Review and meditate on your day and actions
4. Face your shortcomings
5. Ask God for guidance and pray about tomorrow

I'M THANKFUL FOR...

MY SINS & SHORTCOMINGS TODAY

Day 29

O Jesus, through the Immaculate Heart of Mary, I offer You my prayers, works, joys and sufferings of this day for all the intentions of Your Sacred Heart, in union with the Holy Sacrifice of the Mass throughout the world, in reparation for my sins, for the intentions of all my relatives and friends, and in particular for the intentions of the Holy Father. Amen.

Lectio Devina

READ & WRITE IT OUT: BIBLE VERSE

REFLECT: WHAT DOES THIS MEAN TO ME?

RESPOND: WHAT DO I SAY TO GOD ABOUT THIS?

REST IN MEDITATION: HOW IS GOD ASKING ME TO CHANGE?

Examen

1. Ask God to see your day and actions through His eyes
2. Thank Him
3. Review and meditate on your day and actions
4. Face your shortcomings
5. Ask God for guidance and pray about tomorrow

I'M THANKFUL FOR...

MY SINS & SHORTCOMINGS TODAY

Day 30

Morning Prayer

O Jesus, through the Immaculate Heart of Mary, I offer You my prayers, works, joys and sufferings of this day for all the intentions of Your Sacred Heart, in union with the Holy Sacrifice of the Mass throughout the world, in reparation for my sins, for the intentions of all my relatives and friends, and in particular for the intentions of the Holy Father. Amen.

Lectio Devina

READ & WRITE IT: BIBLE VERSE

REFLECT: WHAT DOES THIS MEAN TO ME?

RESPOND: WHAT DO I SAY TO GOD ABOUT THIS?

REST IN MEDITATION: HOW IS GOD ASKING ME TO CHANGE?

Examen

1. Ask God to see your day and actions through His eyes
2. Thank Him
3. Review and meditate on your day and actions
4. Face your shortcomings
5. Ask God for guidance and pray about tomorrow

I'M THANKFUL FOR...

MY SINS & SHORTCOMINGS TODAY

PRAYERS & REFLECTIONS ON YOUR SPIRITUAL JOURNEY THIS MONTH

Jesus, I trust in You!

May

Archbishop Fulton J. Sheen once referred to our Blessed Mother as being like "a magnifying glass that intensifies our love of her Son."

PERSONAL RESOLUTIONS

SPIRITUAL READING LOG

LAST CONFESSION DATE

HOLY ACTIVITIES WITH MY FAMILY/ FRIENDS

PRAYER REQUESTS

✔ ROSARY & CHAPLET TRACKER

"We are all called to be great saints; don't miss the opportunity!" - Mother Angelica

Day 1

O Jesus, through the Immaculate Heart of Mary, I offer You my prayers, works, joys and sufferings of this day for all the intentions of Your Sacred Heart, in union with the Holy Sacrifice of the Mass throughout the world, in reparation for my sins, for the intentions of all my relatives and friends, and in particular for the intentions of the Holy Father. Amen.

Lectio Devina

READ & WRITE IT OUT: BIBLE VERSE

REFLECT: WHAT DOES THIS MEAN TO ME?

RESPOND: WHAT DO I SAY TO GOD ABOUT THIS?

REST IN MEDITATION: HOW IS GOD ASKING ME TO CHANGE?

Examen

1. Ask God to see your day and actions through His eyes
2. Thank Him
3. Review and meditate on your day and actions
4. Face your shortcomings
5. Ask God for guidance and pray about tomorrow

I'M THANKFUL FOR...

MY SINS & SHORTCOMINGS TODAY

Day 2

Morning Prayer

O Jesus, through the Immaculate Heart of Mary, I offer You my prayers, works, joys and sufferings of this day for all the intentions of Your Sacred Heart, in union with the Holy Sacrifice of the Mass throughout the world, in reparation for my sins, for the intentions of all my relatives and friends, and in particular for the intentions of the Holy Father. Amen.

Lect o Devina

READ & WRITE IT: BIBLE VERSE

REFLECT: WHAT DOES THIS MEAN TO ME?

RESPOND: WHAT DO I SAY TO GOD ABOUT THIS?

REST IN MEDITATION: HOW IS GOD ASKING ME TO CHANGE?

Examen

1. Ask God to see your day and actions through His eyes
2. Thank Him
3. Review and meditate on your day and actions
4. Face your shortcomings
5. Ask God for guidance and pray about tomorrow

I'M THANKFUL FOR...

MY SINS & SHORTCOMINGS TODAY

Day 3   *Morning Prayer*

O Jesus, through the Immaculate Heart of Mary, I offer You my prayers, works, joys and sufferings of this day for all the intentions of Your Sacred Heart, in union with the Holy Sacrifice of the Mass throughout the world, in reparation for my sins, for the intentions of all my relatives and friends, and in particular for the intentions of the Holy Father. Amen.

READ & WRITE IT OUT: BIBLE VERSE

REFLECT: WHAT DOES THIS MEAN TO ME?

RESPOND: WHAT DO I SAY TO GOD ABOUT THIS?

REST IN MEDITATION: HOW IS GOD ASKING ME TO CHANGE?

1. Ask God to see your day and actions through His eyes
2. Thank Him
3. Review and meditate on your day and actions
4. Face your shortcomings
5. Ask God for guidance and pray about tomorrow

I'M THANKFUL FOR...

MY SINS & SHORTCOMINGS TODAY

Day 4   *Morning Prayer*

O Jesus, through the Immaculate Heart of Mary, I offer You my prayers, works, joys and sufferings of this day for all the intentions of Your Sacred Heart, in union with the Holy Sacrifice of the Mass throughout the world, in reparation for my sins, for the intentions of all my relatives and friends, and in particular for the intentions of the Holy Father. Amen.

READ & WRITE IT: BIBLE VERSE

REFLECT: WHAT DOES THIS MEAN TO ME?

RESPOND: WHAT DO I SAY TO GOD ABOUT THIS?

REST IN MEDITATION: HOW IS GOD ASKING ME TO CHANGE?

1. Ask God to see your day and actions through His eyes
2. Thank Him
3. Review and meditate on your day and actions
4. Face your shortcomings
5. Ask God for guidance and pray about tomorrow

I'M THANKFUL FOR...

MY SINS & SHORTCOMINGS TODAY

Lectio Devina

Examen

Lectio Devina

Examen

Day 5

Morning Prayer

O Jesus, through the Immaculate Heart of Mary, I offer You my prayers, works, joys and sufferings of this day for all the intentions of Your Sacred Heart, in union with the Holy Sacrifice of the Mass throughout the world, in reparation for my sins, for the intentions of all my relatives and friends, and in particular for the intentions of the Holy Father. Amen.

Lectio Devina

READ & WRITE IT OUT: BIBLE VERSE

REFLECT: WHAT DOES THIS MEAN TO ME?

RESPOND: WHAT DO I SAY TO GOD ABOUT THIS?

REST IN MEDITATION: HOW IS GOD ASKING ME TO CHANGE?

Examen

1. Ask God to see your day and actions through His eyes
2. Thank Him
3. Review and meditate on your day and actions
4. Face your shortcomings
5. Ask God for guidance and pray about tomorrow

I'M THANKFUL FOR...

MY SINS & SHORTCOMINGS TODAY

Day 6

Morning Prayer

O Jesus, through the Immaculate Heart of Mary, I offer You my prayers, works, joys and sufferings of this day for all the intentions of Your Sacred Heart, in union with the Holy Sacrifice of the Mass throughout the world, in reparation for my sins, for the intentions of all my relatives and friends, and in particular for the intentions of the Holy Father. Amen.

Lectio Devina

READ & WRITE IT: BIBLE VERSE

REFLECT: WHAT DOES THIS MEAN TO ME?

RESPOND: WHAT DO I SAY TO GOD ABOUT THIS?

REST IN MEDITATION: HOW IS GOD ASKING ME TO CHANGE?

Examen

1. Ask God to see your day and actions through His eyes
2. Thank Him
3. Review and meditate on your day and actions
4. Face your shortcomings
5. Ask God for guidance and pray about tomorrow

I'M THANKFUL FOR...

MY SINS & SHORTCOMINGS TODAY

Day 7   *Morning Prayer*

O Jesus, through the Immaculate Heart of Mary, I offer You my prayers, works, joys and sufferings of this day for all the intentions of Your Sacred Heart, in union with the Holy Sacrifice of the Mass throughout the world, in reparation for my sins, for the intentions of all my relatives and friends, and in particular for the intentions of the Holy Father. Amen.

READ & WRITE IT OUT: BIBLE VERSE

REFLECT: WHAT DOES THIS MEAN TO ME?

RESPOND: WHAT DO I SAY TO GOD ABOUT THIS?

REST IN MEDITATION: HOW IS GOD ASKING ME TO CHANGE?

Lectio Devina

1. Ask God to see your day and actions through His eyes
2. Thank Him
3. Review and meditate on your day and actions
4. Face your shortcomings
5. Ask God for guidance and pray about tomorrow

I'M THANKFUL FOR...

MY SINS & SHORTCOMINGS TODAY

Examen

Day 8   *Morning Prayer*

O Jesus, through the Immaculate Heart of Mary, I offer You my prayers, works, joys and sufferings of this day for all the intentions of Your Sacred Heart, in union with the Holy Sacrifice of the Mass throughout the world, in reparation for my sins, for the intentions of all my relatives and friends, and in particular for the intentions of the Holy Father. Amen.

READ & WRITE IT: BIBLE VERSE

REFLECT: WHAT DOES THIS MEAN TO ME?

RESPOND: WHAT DO I SAY TO GOD ABOUT THIS?

REST IN MEDITATION: HOW IS GOD ASKING ME TO CHANGE?

Lectio Devina

1. Ask God to see your day and actions through His eyes
2. Thank Him
3. Review and meditate on your day and actions
4. Face your shortcomings
5. Ask God for guidance and pray about tomorrow

I'M THANKFUL FOR...

MY SINS & SHORTCOMINGS TODAY

Examen

Day 9

Morning Prayer

O Jesus, through the Immaculate Heart of Mary, I offer You my prayers, works, joys and sufferings of this day for all the intentions of Your Sacred Heart, in union with the Holy Sacrifice of the Mass throughout the world, in reparation for my sins, for the intentions of all my relatives and friends, and in particular for the intentions of the Holy Father. Amen.

Lectio Devina

READ & WRITE IT OUT: BIBLE VERSE

REFLECT: WHAT DOES THIS MEAN TO ME?

RESPOND: WHAT DO I SAY TO GOD ABOUT THIS?

REST IN MEDITATION: HOW IS GOD ASKING ME TO CHANGE?

Examen

1. Ask God to see your day and actions through His eyes
2. Thank Him
3. Review and meditate on your day and actions
4. Face your shortcomings
5. Ask God for guidance and pray about tomorrow

I'M THANKFUL FOR...

MY SINS & SHORTCOMINGS TODAY

Day 10

Morning Prayer

O Jesus, through the Immaculate Heart of Mary, I offer You my prayers, works, joys and sufferings of this day for all the intentions of Your Sacred Heart, in union with the Holy Sacrifice of the Mass throughout the world, in reparation for my sins, for the intentions of all my relatives and friends, and in particular for the intentions of the Holy Father. Amen.

Lectio Devina

READ & WRITE IT: BIBLE VERSE

REFLECT: WHAT DOES THIS MEAN TO ME?

RESPOND: WHAT DO I SAY TO GOD ABOUT THIS?

REST IN MEDITATION: HOW IS GOD ASKING ME TO CHANGE?

Examen

1. Ask God to see your day and actions through His eyes
2. Thank Him
3. Review and meditate on your day and actions
4. Face your shortcomings
5. Ask God for guidance and pray about tomorrow

I'M THANKFUL FOR...

MY SINS & SHORTCOMINGS TODAY

Day 11   *Morning Prayer*

O Jesus, through the Immaculate Heart of Mary, I offer You my prayers, works, joys and sufferings of this day for all the intentions of Your Sacred Heart, in union with the Holy Sacrifice of the Mass throughout the world, in reparation for my sins, for the intentions of all my relatives and friends, and in particular for the intentions of the Holy Father. Amen.

READ & WRITE IT OUT: BIBLE VERSE

REFLECT: WHAT DOES THIS MEAN TO ME?

RESPOND: WHAT DO I SAY TO GOD ABOUT THIS?

REST IN MEDITATION: HOW IS GOD ASKING ME TO CHANGE?

Lectio Devina

1. Ask God to see your day and actions through His eyes
2. Thank Him
3. Review and meditate on your day and actions
4. Face your shortcomings
5. Ask God for guidance and pray about tomorrow

I'M THANKFUL FOR...

MY SINS & SHORTCOMINGS TODAY

Examen

Day 12   *Morning Prayer*

O Jesus, through the Immaculate Heart of Mary, I offer You my prayers, works, joys and sufferings of this day for all the intentions of Your Sacred Heart, in union with the Holy Sacrifice of the Mass throughout the world, in reparation for my sins, for the intentions of all my relatives and friends, and in particular for the intentions of the Holy Father. Amen.

READ & WRITE IT: BIBLE VERSE

REFLECT: WHAT DOES THIS MEAN TO ME?

RESPOND: WHAT DO I SAY TO GOD ABOUT THIS?

REST IN MEDITATION: HOW IS GOD ASKING ME TO CHANGE?

Lectio Devina

1. Ask God to see your day and actions through His eyes
2. Thank Him
3. Review and meditate on your day and actions
4. Face your shortcomings
5. Ask God for guidance and pray about tomorrow

I'M THANKFUL FOR...

MY SINS & SHORTCOMINGS TODAY

Examen

Day 13   *Morning Prayer*

O Jesus, through the Immaculate Heart of Mary, I offer You my prayers, works, joys and sufferings of this day for all the intentions of Your Sacred Heart, in union with the Holy Sacrifice of the Mass throughout the world, in reparation for my sins, for the intentions of all my relatives and friends, and in particular for the intentions of the Holy Father. Amen.

READ & WRITE IT OUT: BIBLE VERSE

Lectio Devina

REFLECT: WHAT DOES THIS MEAN TO ME?

RESPOND: WHAT DO I SAY TO GOD ABOUT THIS?

REST IN MEDITATION: HOW IS GOD ASKING ME TO CHANGE?

Examen

1. Ask God to see your day and actions through His eyes
2. Thank Him
3. Review and meditate on your day and actions
4. Face your shortcomings
5. Ask God for guidance and pray about tomorrow

I'M THANKFUL FOR...   MY SINS & SHORTCOMINGS TODAY

Day 14   *Morning Prayer*

O Jesus, through the Immaculate Heart of Mary, I offer You my prayers, works, joys and sufferings of this day for all the intentions of Your Sacred Heart, in union with the Holy Sacrifice of the Mass throughout the world, in reparation for my sins, for the intentions of all my relatives and friends, and in particular for the intentions of the Holy Father. Amen.

READ & WRITE IT: BIBLE VERSE

Lectio Devina

REFLECT: WHAT DOES THIS MEAN TO ME?

RESPOND: WHAT DO I SAY TO GOD ABOUT THIS?

REST IN MEDITATION: HOW IS GOD ASKING ME TO CHANGE?

Examen

1. Ask God to see your day and actions through His eyes
2. Thank Him
3. Review and meditate on your day and actions
4. Face your shortcomings
5. Ask God for guidance and pray about tomorrow

I'M THANKFUL FOR...   MY SINS & SHORTCOMINGS TODAY

Day 15

Morning Prayer

Morning Prayer

O Jesus, through the Immaculate Heart of Mary, I offer You my prayers, works, joys and sufferings of this day for all the intentions of Your Sacred Heart, in union with the Holy Sacrifice of the Mass throughout the world, in reparation for my sins, for the intentions of all my relatives and friends, and in particular for the intentions of the Holy Father. Amen.

Lectio Devina

READ & WRITE IT OUT: BIBLE VERSE

REFLECT: WHAT DOES THIS MEAN TO ME?

RESPOND: WHAT DO I SAY TO GOD ABOUT THIS?

REST IN MEDITATION: HOW IS GOD ASKING ME TO CHANGE?

Examen

1. Ask God to see your day and actions through His eyes
2. Thank Him
3. Review and meditate on your day and actions
4. Face your shortcomings
5. Ask God for guidance and pray about tomorrow

I'M THANKFUL FOR...

MY SINS & SHORTCOMINGS TODAY

Day 16

Morning Prayer

O Jesus, through the Immaculate Heart of Mary, I offer You my prayers, works, joys and sufferings of this day for all the intentions of Your Sacred Heart, in union with the Holy Sacrifice of the Mass throughout the world, in reparation for my sins, for the intentions of all my relatives and friends, and in particular for the intentions of the Holy Father. Amen.

Lectio Devina

READ & WRITE IT: BIBLE VERSE

REFLECT: WHAT DOES THIS MEAN TO ME?

RESPOND: WHAT DO I SAY TO GOD ABOUT THIS?

REST IN MEDITATION: HOW IS GOD ASKING ME TO CHANGE?

Examen

1. Ask God to see your day and actions through His eyes
2. Thank Him
3. Review and meditate on your day and actions
4. Face your shortcomings
5. Ask God for guidance and pray about tomorrow

I'M THANKFUL FOR...

MY SINS & SHORTCOMINGS TODAY

Day 17   *Morning Prayer*

O Jesus, through the Immaculate Heart of Mary, I offer You my prayers, works, joys and sufferings of this day for all the intentions of Your Sacred Heart, in union with the Holy Sacrifice of the Mass throughout the world, in reparation for my sins, for the intentions of all my relatives and friends, and in particular for the intentions of the Holy Father. Amen.

READ & WRITE IT OUT: BIBLE VERSE

REFLECT: WHAT DOES THIS MEAN TO ME?

RESPOND: WHAT DO I SAY TO GOD ABOUT THIS?

REST IN MEDITATION: HOW IS GOD ASKING ME TO CHANGE?

Lectio Devina

1. Ask God to see your day and actions through His eyes
2. Thank Him
3. Review and meditate on your day and actions
4. Face your shortcomings
5. Ask God for guidance and pray about tomorrow

I'M THANKFUL FOR...

MY SINS & SHORTCOMINGS TODAY

Examen

Day 18   *Morning Prayer*

O Jesus, through the Immaculate Heart of Mary, I offer You my prayers, works, joys and sufferings of this day for all the intentions of Your Sacred Heart, in union with the Holy Sacrifice of the Mass throughout the world, in reparation for my sins, for the intentions of all my relatives and friends, and in particular for the intentions of the Holy Father. Amen.

READ & WRITE IT: BIBLE VERSE

REFLECT: WHAT DOES THIS MEAN TO ME?

RESPOND: WHAT DO I SAY TO GOD ABOUT THIS?

REST IN MEDITATION: HOW IS GOD ASKING ME TO CHANGE?

Lectio Devina

1. Ask God to see your day and actions through His eyes
2. Thank Him
3. Review and meditate on your day and actions
4. Face your shortcomings
5. Ask God for guidance and pray about tomorrow

I'M THANKFUL FOR...

MY SINS & SHORTCOMINGS TODAY

Examen

Day 19   *Morning Prayer*

O Jesus, through the Immaculate Heart of Mary, I offer You my prayers, works, joys and sufferings of this day for all the intentions of Your Sacred Heart, in union with the Holy Sacrifice of the Mass throughout the world, in reparation for my sins, for the intentions of all my relatives and friends, and in particular for the intentions of the Holy Father. Amen.

READ & WRITE IT OUT: BIBLE VERSE

REFLECT: WHAT DOES THIS MEAN TO ME?

RESPOND: WHAT DO I SAY TO GOD ABOUT THIS?

REST IN MEDITATION: HOW IS GOD ASKING ME TO CHANGE?

Lectio Devina

1. Ask God to see your day and actions through His eyes
2. Thank Him
3. Review and meditate on your day and actions
4. Face your shortcomings
5. Ask God for guidance and pray about tomorrow

I'M THANKFUL FOR...

MY SINS & SHORTCOMINGS TODAY

Examen

Day 20   *Morning Prayer*

O Jesus, through the Immaculate Heart of Mary, I offer You my prayers, works, joys and sufferings of this day for all the intentions of Your Sacred Heart, in union with the Holy Sacrifice of the Mass throughout the world, in reparation for my sins, for the intentions of all my relatives and friends, and in particular for the intentions of the Holy Father. Amen.

READ & WRITE IT: BIBLE VERSE

REFLECT: WHAT DOES THIS MEAN TO ME?

RESPOND: WHAT DO I SAY TO GOD ABOUT THIS?

REST IN MEDITATION: HOW IS GOD ASKING ME TO CHANGE?

Lectio Devina

1. Ask God to see your day and actions through His eyes
2. Thank Him
3. Review and meditate on your day and actions
4. Face your shortcomings
5. Ask God for guidance and pray about tomorrow

I'M THANKFUL FOR...

MY SINS & SHORTCOMINGS TODAY

Examen

Day 21

O Jesus, through the Immaculate Heart of Mary, I offer You my prayers, works, joys and sufferings of this day for all the intentions of Your Sacred Heart, in union with the Holy Sacrifice of the Mass throughout the world, in reparation for my sins, for the intentions of all my relatives and friends, and in particular for the intentions of the Holy Father. Amen.

Lectio Devina

READ & WRITE IT OUT: BIBLE VERSE

REFLECT: WHAT DOES THIS MEAN TO ME?

RESPOND: WHAT DO I SAY TO GOD ABOUT THIS?

REST IN MEDITATION: HOW IS GOD ASKING ME TO CHANGE?

Examen

1. Ask God to see your day and actions through His eyes
2. Thank Him
3. Review and meditate on your day and actions
4. Face your shortcomings
5. Ask God for guidance and pray about tomorrow

I'M THANKFUL FOR...

MY SINS & SHORTCOMINGS TODAY

Day 22

Morning Prayer

O Jesus, through the Immaculate Heart of Mary, I offer You my prayers, works, joys and sufferings of this day for all the intentions of Your Sacred Heart, in union with the Holy Sacrifice of the Mass throughout the world, in reparation for my sins, for the intentions of all my relatives and friends, and in particular for the intentions of the Holy Father. Amen.

Lectio Devina

READ & WRITE IT: BIBLE VERSE

REFLECT: WHAT DOES THIS MEAN TO ME?

RESPOND: WHAT DO I SAY TO GOD ABOUT THIS?

REST IN MEDITATION: HOW IS GOD ASKING ME TO CHANGE?

Examen

1. Ask God to see your day and actions through His eyes
2. Thank Him
3. Review and meditate on your day and actions
4. Face your shortcomings
5. Ask God for guidance and pray about tomorrow

I'M THANKFUL FOR...

MY SINS & SHORTCOMINGS TODAY

Day 23   *Morning Prayer*

O Jesus, through the Immaculate Heart of Mary, I offer You my prayers, works, joys and sufferings of this day for all the intentions of Your Sacred Heart, in union with the Holy Sacrifice of the Mass throughout the world, in reparation for my sins, for the intentions of all my relatives and friends, and in particular for the intentions of the Holy Father. Amen.

READ & WRITE IT OUT: BIBLE VERSE

REFLECT: WHAT DOES THIS MEAN TO ME?

RESPOND: WHAT DO I SAY TO GOD ABOUT THIS?

REST IN MEDITATION: HOW IS GOD ASKING ME TO CHANGE?

Lectio Devina

1. Ask God to see your day and actions through His eyes
2. Thank Him
3. Review and meditate on your day and actions
4. Face your shortcomings
5. Ask God for guidance and pray about tomorrow

I'M THANKFUL FOR...

MY SINS & SHORTCOMINGS TODAY

Examen

Day 24   *Morning Prayer*

O Jesus, through the Immaculate Heart of Mary, I offer You my prayers, works, joys and sufferings of this day for all the intentions of Your Sacred Heart, in union with the Holy Sacrifice of the Mass throughout the world, in reparation for my sins, for the intentions of all my relatives and friends, and in particular for the intentions of the Holy Father. Amen.

READ & WRITE IT: BIBLE VERSE

REFLECT: WHAT DOES THIS MEAN TO ME?

RESPOND: WHAT DO I SAY TO GOD ABOUT THIS?

REST IN MEDITATION: HOW IS GOD ASKING ME TO CHANGE?

Lectio Devina

1. Ask God to see your day and actions through His eyes
2. Thank Him
3. Review and meditate on your day and actions
4. Face your shortcomings
5. Ask God for guidance and pray about tomorrow

I'M THANKFUL FOR...

MY SINS & SHORTCOMINGS TODAY

Examen

Day 25

Morning Prayer

O Jesus, through the Immaculate Heart of Mary, I offer You my prayers, works, joys and sufferings of this day for all the intentions of Your Sacred Heart, in union with the Holy Sacrifice of the Mass throughout the world, in reparation for my sins, for the intentions of all my relatives and friends, and in particular for the intentions of the Holy Father. Amen.

Lectio Devina

READ & WRITE IT OUT: BIBLE VERSE

REFLECT: WHAT DOES THIS MEAN TO ME?

RESPOND: WHAT DO I SAY TO GOD ABOUT THIS?

REST IN MEDITATION: HOW IS GOD ASKING ME TO CHANGE?

Examen

1. Ask God to see your day and actions through His eyes
2. Thank Him
3. Review and meditate on your day and actions
4. Face your shortcomings
5. Ask God for guidance and pray about tomorrow

I'M THANKFUL FOR...

MY SINS & SHORTCOMINGS TODAY

Day 26

Morning Prayer

O Jesus, through the Immaculate Heart of Mary, I offer You my prayers, works, joys and sufferings of this day for all the intentions of Your Sacred Heart, in union with the Holy Sacrifice of the Mass throughout the world, in reparation for my sins, for the intentions of all my relatives and friends, and in particular for the intentions of the Holy Father. Amen.

Lectio Devina

READ & WRITE IT: BIBLE VERSE

REFLECT: WHAT DOES THIS MEAN TO ME?

RESPOND: WHAT DO I SAY TO GOD ABOUT THIS?

REST IN MEDITATION: HOW IS GOD ASKING ME TO CHANGE?

Examen

1. Ask God to see your day and actions through His eyes
2. Thank Him
3. Review and meditate on your day and actions
4. Face your shortcomings
5. Ask God for guidance and pray about tomorrow

I'M THANKFUL FOR...

MY SINS & SHORTCOMINGS TODAY

Day 27

O Jesus, through the Immaculate Heart of Mary, I offer You my prayers, works, joys and sufferings of this day for all the intentions of Your Sacred Heart, in union with the Holy Sacrifice of the Mass throughout the world, in reparation for my sins, for the intentions of all my relatives and friends, and in particular for the intentions of the Holy Father. Amen.

READ & WRITE IT OUT: BIBLE VERSE

Lectio Devina

REFLECT: WHAT DOES THIS MEAN TO ME?

RESPOND: WHAT DO I SAY TO GOD ABOUT THIS?

REST IN MEDITATION: HOW IS GOD ASKING ME TO CHANGE?

Examen

1. Ask God to see your day and actions through His eyes
2. Thank Him
3. Review and meditate on your day and actions
4. Face your shortcomings
5. Ask God for guidance and pray about tomorrow

I'M THANKFUL FOR...

MY SINS & SHORTCOMINGS TODAY

Day 28

Morning Prayer

O Jesus, through the Immaculate Heart of Mary, I offer You my prayers, works, joys and sufferings of this day for all the intentions of Your Sacred Heart, in union with the Holy Sacrifice of the Mass throughout the world, in reparation for my sins, for the intentions of all my relatives and friends, and in particular for the intentions of the Holy Father. Amen.

READ & WRITE IT: BIBLE VERSE

Lectio Devina

REFLECT: WHAT DOES THIS MEAN TO ME?

RESPOND: WHAT DO I SAY TO GOD ABOUT THIS?

REST IN MEDITATION: HOW IS GOD ASKING ME TO CHANGE?

Examen

1. Ask God to see your day and actions through His eyes
2. Thank Him
3. Review and meditate on your day and actions
4. Face your shortcomings
5. Ask God for guidance and pray about tomorrow

I'M THANKFUL FOR...

MY SINS & SHORTCOMINGS TODAY

Day 29

O Jesus, through the Immaculate Heart of Mary, I offer You my prayers, works, joys and sufferings of this day for all the intentions of Your Sacred Heart, in union with the Holy Sacrifice of the Mass throughout the world, in reparation for my sins, for the intentions of all my relatives and friends, and in particular for the intentions of the Holy Father. Amen.

Lectio Devina

READ & WRITE IT OUT: BIBLE VERSE

REFLECT: WHAT DOES THIS MEAN TO ME?

RESPOND: WHAT DO I SAY TO GOD ABOUT THIS?

REST IN MEDITATION: HOW IS GOD ASKING ME TO CHANGE?

Examen

1. Ask God to see your day and actions through His eyes
2. Thank Him
3. Review and meditate on your day and actions
4. Face your shortcomings
5. Ask God for guidance and pray about tomorrow

I'M THANKFUL FOR...

MY SINS & SHORTCOMINGS TODAY

Day 30

Morning Prayer

O Jesus, through the Immaculate Heart of Mary, I offer You my prayers, works, joys and sufferings of this day for all the intentions of Your Sacred Heart, in union with the Holy Sacrifice of the Mass throughout the world, in reparation for my sins, for the intentions of all my relatives and friends, and in particular for the intentions of the Holy Father. Amen.

Lectio Devina

READ & WRITE IT: BIBLE VERSE

REFLECT: WHAT DOES THIS MEAN TO ME?

RESPOND: WHAT DO I SAY TO GOD ABOUT THIS?

REST IN MEDITATION: HOW IS GOD ASKING ME TO CHANGE?

Examen

1. Ask God to see your day and actions through His eyes
2. Thank Him
3. Review and meditate on your day and actions
4. Face your shortcomings
5. Ask God for guidance and pray about tomorrow

I'M THANKFUL FOR...

MY SINS & SHORTCOMINGS TODAY

Day 31   *Morning Prayer*

O Jesus, through the Immaculate Heart of Mary, I offer You my prayers, works, joys and sufferings of this day for all the intentions of Your Sacred Heart, in union with the Holy Sacrifice of the Mass throughout the world, in reparation for my sins, for the intentions of all my relatives and friends, and in particular for the intentions of the Holy Father. Amen.

Lectio Devina

READ & WRITE IT OUT: BIBLE VERSE

REFLECT: WHAT DOES THIS MEAN TO ME?

RESPOND: WHAT DO I SAY TO GOD ABOUT THIS?

REST IN MEDITATION: HOW IS GOD ASKING ME TO CHANGE?

Examen

1. Ask God to see your day and actions through His eyes
2. Thank Him
3. Review and meditate on your day and actions
4. Face your shortcomings
5. Ask God for guidance and pray about tomorrow

I'M THANKFUL FOR...

MY SINS & SHORTCOMINGS TODAY

PRAYERS & REFLECTIONS ON YOUR SPIRITUAL JOURNEY THIS MONTH

June

"The Heart of Jesus is the ultimate symbol of God's Mercy; but it is not an imaginary symbol. It is a real symbol, which represents the center, the source from which salvation for all humanity gushed forth." -Pope Francis

PERSONAL RESOLUTIONS

SPIRITUAL READING LOG

LAST CONFESSION DATE

HOLY ACTIVITIES WITH MY FAMILY/ FRIENDS

PRAYER REQUESTS

ROSARY & CHAPLET TRACKER

"We are all called to be great saints; don't miss the opportunity!" - Mother Angelica

Day 1

Morning Prayer

O Jesus, through the Immaculate Heart of Mary, I offer You my prayers, works, joys and sufferings of this day for all the intentions of Your Sacred Heart, in union with the Holy Sacrifice of the Mass throughout the world, in reparation for my sins, for the intentions of all my relatives and friends, and in particular for the intentions of the Holy Father. Amen.

READ & WRITE IT OUT: BIBLE VERSE

REFLECT: WHAT DOES THIS MEAN TO ME?

RESPOND: WHAT DO I SAY TO GOD ABOUT THIS?

REST IN MEDITATION: HOW IS GOD ASKING ME TO CHANGE?

Lectio Devina

1. Ask God to see your day and actions through His eyes
2. Thank Him
3. Review and meditate on your day and actions
4. Face your shortcomings
5. Ask God for guidance and pray about tomorrow

Examen

I'M THANKFUL FOR...

MY SINS & SHORTCOMINGS TODAY

Day 2

Morning Prayer

O Jesus, through the Immaculate Heart of Mary, I offer You my prayers, works, joys and sufferings of this day for all the intentions of Your Sacred Heart, in union with the Holy Sacrifice of the Mass throughout the world, in reparation for my sins, for the intentions of all my relatives and friends, and in particular for the intentions of the Holy Father. Amen.

READ & WRITE IT: BIBLE VERSE

REFLECT: WHAT DOES THIS MEAN TO ME?

RESPOND: WHAT DO I SAY TO GOD ABOUT THIS?

REST IN MEDITATION: HOW IS GOD ASKING ME TO CHANGE?

Lectio Devina

1. Ask God to see your day and actions through His eyes
2. Thank Him
3. Review and meditate on your day and actions
4. Face your shortcomings
5. Ask God for guidance and pray about tomorrow

Examen

I'M THANKFUL FOR...

MY SINS & SHORTCOMINGS TODAY

Day 3

O Jesus, through the Immaculate Heart of Mary, I offer You my prayers, works, joys and sufferings of this day for all the intentions of Your Sacred Heart, in union with the Holy Sacrifice of the Mass throughout the world, in reparation for my sins, for the intentions of all my relatives and friends, and in particular for the intentions of the Holy Father. Amen.

READ & WRITE IT OUT: BIBLE VERSE

Lectio Devina

REFLECT: WHAT DOES THIS MEAN TO ME?

RESPOND: WHAT DO I SAY TO GOD ABOUT THIS?

REST IN MEDITATION: HOW IS GOD ASKING ME TO CHANGE?

Examen

1. Ask God to see your day and actions through His eyes
2. Thank Him
3. Review and meditate on your day and actions
4. Face your shortcomings
5. Ask God for guidance and pray about tomorrow

I'M THANKFUL FOR...

MY SINS & SHORTCOMINGS TODAY

Day 4

Morning Prayer

O Jesus, through the Immaculate Heart of Mary, I offer You my prayers, works, joys and sufferings of this day for all the intentions of Your Sacred Heart, in union with the Holy Sacrifice of the Mass throughout the world, in reparation for my sins, for the intentions of all my relatives and friends, and in particular for the intentions of the Holy Father. Amen.

READ & WRITE IT: BIBLE VERSE

Lectio Devina

REFLECT: WHAT DOES THIS MEAN TO ME?

RESPOND: WHAT DO I SAY TO GOD ABOUT THIS?

REST IN MEDITATION: HOW IS GOD ASKING ME TO CHANGE?

Examen

1. Ask God to see your day and actions through His eyes
2. Thank Him
3. Review and meditate on your day and actions
4. Face your shortcomings
5. Ask God for guidance and pray about tomorrow

I'M THANKFUL FOR...

MY SINS & SHORTCOMINGS TODAY

Day 5   *Morning Prayer*

O Jesus, through the Immaculate Heart of Mary, I offer You my prayers, works, joys and sufferings of this day for all the intentions of Your Sacred Heart, in union with the Holy Sacrifice of the Mass throughout the world, in reparation for my sins, for the intentions of all my relatives and friends, and in particular for the intentions of the Holy Father. Amen.

Lectio Devina

READ & WRITE IT OUT: BIBLE VERSE

REFLECT: WHAT DOES THIS MEAN TO ME?

RESPOND: WHAT DO I SAY TO GOD ABOUT THIS?

REST IN MEDITATION: HOW IS GOD ASKING ME TO CHANGE?

Examen

1. Ask God to see your day and actions through His eyes
2. Thank Him
3. Review and meditate on your day and actions
4. Face your shortcomings
5. Ask God for guidance and pray about tomorrow

I'M THANKFUL FOR...

MY SINS & SHORTCOMINGS TODAY

Day 6   *Morning Prayer*

O Jesus, through the Immaculate Heart of Mary, I offer You my prayers, works, joys and sufferings of this day for all the intentions of Your Sacred Heart, in union with the Holy Sacrifice of the Mass throughout the world, in reparation for my sins, for the intentions of all my relatives and friends, and in particular for the intentions of the Holy Father. Amen.

Lectio Devina

READ & WRITE IT: BIBLE VERSE

REFLECT: WHAT DOES THIS MEAN TO ME?

RESPOND: WHAT DO I SAY TO GOD ABOUT THIS?

REST IN MEDITATION: HOW IS GOD ASKING ME TO CHANGE?

Examen

1. Ask God to see your day and actions through His eyes
2. Thank Him
3. Review and meditate on your day and actions
4. Face your shortcomings
5. Ask God for guidance and pray about tomorrow

I'M THANKFUL FOR...

MY SINS & SHORTCOMINGS TODAY

Day 7

O Jesus, through the Immaculate Heart of Mary, I offer You my prayers, works, joys and sufferings of this day for all the intentions of Your Sacred Heart, in union with the Holy Sacrifice of the Mass throughout the world, in reparation for my sins, for the intentions of all my relatives and friends, and in particular for the intentions of the Holy Father. Amen.

Lectio Devina

READ & WRITE IT OUT: BIBLE VERSE

REFLECT: WHAT DOES THIS MEAN TO ME?

RESPOND: WHAT DO I SAY TO GOD ABOUT THIS?

REST IN MEDITATION: HOW IS GOD ASKING ME TO CHANGE?

Examen

1. Ask God to see your day and actions through His eyes
2. Thank Him
3. Review and meditate on your day and actions
4. Face your shortcomings
5. Ask God for guidance and pray about tomorrow

I'M THANKFUL FOR...

MY SINS & SHORTCOMINGS TODAY

Day 8

Morning Prayer

O Jesus, through the Immaculate Heart of Mary, I offer You my prayers, works, joys and sufferings of this day for all the intentions of Your Sacred Heart, in union with the Holy Sacrifice of the Mass throughout the world, in reparation for my sins, for the intentions of all my relatives and friends, and in particular for the intentions of the Holy Father. Amen.

Lectio Devina

READ & WRITE IT: BIBLE VERSE

REFLECT: WHAT DOES THIS MEAN TO ME?

RESPOND: WHAT DO I SAY TO GOD ABOUT THIS?

REST IN MEDITATION: HOW IS GOD ASKING ME TO CHANGE?

Examen

1. Ask God to see your day and actions through His eyes
2. Thank Him
3. Review and meditate on your day and actions
4. Face your shortcomings
5. Ask God for guidance and pray about tomorrow

I'M THANKFUL FOR...

MY SINS & SHORTCOMINGS TODAY

Day 9   *Morning Prayer*

O Jesus, through the Immaculate Heart of Mary, I offer You my prayers, works, joys and sufferings of this day for all the intentions of Your Sacred Heart, in union with the Holy Sacrifice of the Mass throughout the world, in reparation for my sins, for the intentions of all my relatives and friends, and in particular for the intentions of the Holy Father. Amen.

READ & WRITE IT OUT: BIBLE VERSE

REFLECT: WHAT DOES THIS MEAN TO ME?

RESPOND: WHAT DO I SAY TO GOD ABOUT THIS?

REST IN MEDITATION: HOW IS GOD ASKING ME TO CHANGE?

1. Ask God to see your day and actions through His eyes
2. Thank Him
3. Review and meditate on your day and actions
4. Face your shortcomings
5. Ask God for guidance and pray about tomorrow

I'M THANKFUL FOR...

MY SINS & SHORTCOMINGS TODAY

Day 10   *Morning Prayer*

O Jesus, through the Immaculate Heart of Mary, I offer You my prayers, works, joys and sufferings of this day for all the intentions of Your Sacred Heart, in union with the Holy Sacrifice of the Mass throughout the world, in reparation for my sins, for the intentions of all my relatives and friends, and in particular for the intentions of the Holy Father. Amen.

READ & WRITE IT: BIBLE VERSE

REFLECT: WHAT DOES THIS MEAN TO ME?

RESPOND: WHAT DO I SAY TO GOD ABOUT THIS?

REST IN MEDITATION: HOW IS GOD ASKING ME TO CHANGE?

1. Ask God to see your day and actions through His eyes
2. Thank Him
3. Review and meditate on your day and actions
4. Face your shortcomings
5. Ask God for guidance and pray about tomorrow

I'M THANKFUL FOR...

MY SINS & SHORTCOMINGS TODAY

Day 11

Morning Prayer

O Jesus, through the Immaculate Heart of Mary, I offer You my prayers, works, joys and sufferings of this day for all the intentions of Your Sacred Heart, in union with the Holy Sacrifice of the Mass throughout the world, in reparation for my sins, for the intentions of all my relatives and friends, and in particular for the intentions of the Holy Father. Amen.

Lectio Devina

READ & WRITE IT OUT: BIBLE VERSE

REFLECT: WHAT DOES THIS MEAN TO ME?

RESPOND: WHAT DO I SAY TO GOD ABOUT THIS?

REST IN MEDITATION: HOW IS GOD ASKING ME TO CHANGE?

Examen

1. Ask God to see your day and actions through His eyes
2. Thank Him
3. Review and meditate on your day and actions
4. Face your shortcomings
5. Ask God for guidance and pray about tomorrow

I'M THANKFUL FOR...

MY SINS & SHORTCOMINGS TODAY

Day 12

Morning Prayer

O Jesus, through the Immaculate Heart of Mary, I offer You my prayers, works, joys and sufferings of this day for all the intentions of Your Sacred Heart, in union with the Holy Sacrifice of the Mass throughout the world, in reparation for my sins, for the intentions of all my relatives and friends, and in particular for the intentions of the Holy Father. Amen.

Lectio Devina

READ & WRITE IT: BIBLE VERSE

REFLECT: WHAT DOES THIS MEAN TO ME?

RESPOND: WHAT DO I SAY TO GOD ABOUT THIS?

REST IN MEDITATION: HOW IS GOD ASKING ME TO CHANGE?

Examen

1. Ask God to see your day and actions through His eyes
2. Thank Him
3. Review and meditate on your day and actions
4. Face your shortcomings
5. Ask God for guidance and pray about tomorrow

I'M THANKFUL FOR...

MY SINS & SHORTCOMINGS TODAY

Day 13

Morning Prayer

O Jesus, through the Immaculate Heart of Mary, I offer You my prayers, works, joys and sufferings of this day for all the intentions of Your Sacred Heart, in union with the Holy Sacrifice of the Mass throughout the world, in reparation for my sins, for the intentions of all my relatives and friends, and in particular for the intentions of the Holy Father. Amen.

Lectio Devina

READ & WRITE IT OUT: BIBLE VERSE

REFLECT: WHAT DOES THIS MEAN TO ME?

RESPOND: WHAT DO I SAY TO GOD ABOUT THIS?

REST IN MEDITATION: HOW IS GOD ASKING ME TO CHANGE?

Examen

1. Ask God to see your day and actions through His eyes
2. Thank Him
3. Review and meditate on your day and actions
4. Face your shortcomings
5. Ask God for guidance and pray about tomorrow

I'M THANKFUL FOR...

MY SINS & SHORTCOMINGS TODAY

Day 14

Morning Prayer

O Jesus, through the Immaculate Heart of Mary, I offer You my prayers, works, joys and sufferings of this day for all the intentions of Your Sacred Heart, in union with the Holy Sacrifice of the Mass throughout the world, in reparation for my sins, for the intentions of all my relatives and friends, and in particular for the intentions of the Holy Father. Amen.

Lectio Devina

READ & WRITE IT: BIBLE VERSE

REFLECT: WHAT DOES THIS MEAN TO ME?

RESPOND: WHAT DO I SAY TO GOD ABOUT THIS?

REST IN MEDITATION: HOW IS GOD ASKING ME TO CHANGE?

Examen

1. Ask God to see your day and actions through His eyes
2. Thank Him
3. Review and meditate on your day and actions
4. Face your shortcomings
5. Ask God for guidance and pray about tomorrow

I'M THANKFUL FOR...

MY SINS & SHORTCOMINGS TODAY

Day 15

O Jesus, through the Immaculate Heart of Mary, I offer You my prayers, works, joys and sufferings of this day for all the intentions of Your Sacred Heart, in union with the Holy Sacrifice of the Mass throughout the world, in reparation for my sins, for the intentions of all my relatives and friends, and in particular for the intentions of the Holy Father. Amen.

Lectio Devina

READ & WRITE IT OUT: BIBLE VERSE

REFLECT: WHAT DOES THIS MEAN TO ME?

RESPOND: WHAT DO I SAY TO GOD ABOUT THIS?

REST IN MEDITATION: HOW IS GOD ASKING ME TO CHANGE?

Examen

1. Ask God to see your day and actions through His eyes
2. Thank Him
3. Review and meditate on your day and actions
4. Face your shortcomings
5. Ask God for guidance and pray about tomorrow

I'M THANKFUL FOR...

MY SINS & SHORTCOMINGS TODAY

Day 16

Morning Prayer

O Jesus, through the Immaculate Heart of Mary, I offer You my prayers, works, joys and sufferings of this day for all the intentions of Your Sacred Heart, in union with the Holy Sacrifice of the Mass throughout the world, in reparation for my sins, for the intentions of all my relatives and friends, and in particular for the intentions of the Holy Father. Amen.

Lectio Devina

READ & WRITE IT: BIBLE VERSE

REFLECT: WHAT DOES THIS MEAN TO ME?

RESPOND: WHAT DO I SAY TO GOD ABOUT THIS?

REST IN MEDITATION: HOW IS GOD ASKING ME TO CHANGE?

Examen

1. Ask God to see your day and actions through His eyes
2. Thank Him
3. Review and meditate on your day and actions
4. Face your shortcomings
5. Ask God for guidance and pray about tomorrow

I'M THANKFUL FOR...

MY SINS & SHORTCOMINGS TODAY

Day 17   *Morning Prayer*

O Jesus, through the Immaculate Heart of Mary, I offer You my prayers, works, joys and sufferings of this day for all the intentions of Your Sacred Heart, in union with the Holy Sacrifice of the Mass throughout the world, in reparation for my sins, for the intentions of all my relatives and friends, and in particular for the intentions of the Holy Father. Amen.

READ & WRITE IT OUT: BIBLE VERSE

REFLECT: WHAT DOES THIS MEAN TO ME?

RESPOND: WHAT DO I SAY TO GOD ABOUT THIS?

REST IN MEDITATION: HOW IS GOD ASKING ME TO CHANGE?

Lectio Devina

1. Ask God to see your day and actions through His eyes
2. Thank Him
3. Review and meditate on your day and actions
4. Face your shortcomings
5. Ask God for guidance and pray about tomorrow

I'M THANKFUL FOR...

MY SINS & SHORTCOMINGS TODAY

Examen

Day 18   *Morning Prayer*

O Jesus, through the Immaculate Heart of Mary, I offer You my prayers, works, joys and sufferings of this day for all the intentions of Your Sacred Heart, in union with the Holy Sacrifice of the Mass throughout the world, in reparation for my sins, for the intentions of all my relatives and friends, and in particular for the intentions of the Holy Father. Amen.

READ & WRITE IT: BIBLE VERSE

REFLECT: WHAT DOES THIS MEAN TO ME?

RESPOND: WHAT DO I SAY TO GOD ABOUT THIS?

REST IN MEDITATION: HOW IS GOD ASKING ME TO CHANGE?

Lectio Devina

1. Ask God to see your day and actions through His eyes
2. Thank Him
3. Review and meditate on your day and actions
4. Face your shortcomings
5. Ask God for guidance and pray about tomorrow

I'M THANKFUL FOR...

MY SINS & SHORTCOMINGS TODAY

Examen

Day 19   *Morning Prayer*

O Jesus, through the Immaculate Heart of Mary, I offer You my prayers, works, joys and sufferings of this day for all the intentions of Your Sacred Heart, in union with the Holy Sacrifice of the Mass throughout the world, in reparation for my sins, for the intentions of all my relatives and friends, and in particular for the intentions of the Holy Father. Amen.

READ & WRITE IT OUT: BIBLE VERSE

Lectio Devina

REFLECT: WHAT DOES THIS MEAN TO ME?

RESPOND: WHAT DO I SAY TO GOD ABOUT THIS?

REST IN MEDITATION: HOW IS GOD ASKING ME TO CHANGE?

Examen

1. Ask God to see your day and actions through His eyes
2. Thank Him
3. Review and meditate on your day and actions
4. Face your shortcomings
5. Ask God for guidance and pray about tomorrow

I'M THANKFUL FOR...   MY SINS & SHORTCOMINGS TODAY

Day 20   *Morning Prayer*

O Jesus, through the Immaculate Heart of Mary, I offer You my prayers, works, joys and sufferings of this day for all the intentions of Your Sacred Heart, in union with the Holy Sacrifice of the Mass throughout the world, in reparation for my sins, for the intentions of all my relatives and friends, and in particular for the intentions of the Holy Father. Amen.

READ & WRITE IT: BIBLE VERSE

Lectio Devina

REFLECT: WHAT DOES THIS MEAN TO ME?

RESPOND: WHAT DO I SAY TO GOD ABOUT THIS?

REST IN MEDITATION: HOW IS GOD ASKING ME TO CHANGE?

Examen

1. Ask God to see your day and actions through His eyes
2. Thank Him
3. Review and meditate on your day and actions
4. Face your shortcomings
5. Ask God for guidance and pray about tomorrow

I'M THANKFUL FOR...   MY SINS & SHORTCOMINGS TODAY

Day 21

O Jesus, through the Immaculate Heart of Mary, I offer You my prayers, works, joys and sufferings of this day for all the intentions of Your Sacred Heart, in union with the Holy Sacrifice of the Mass throughout the world, in reparation for my sins, for the intentions of all my relatives and friends, and in particular for the intentions of the Holy Father. Amen.

Lectio Devina

READ & WRITE IT OUT: BIBLE VERSE

REFLECT: WHAT DOES THIS MEAN TO ME?

RESPOND: WHAT DO I SAY TO GOD ABOUT THIS?

REST IN MEDITATION: HOW IS GOD ASKING ME TO CHANGE?

Examen

1. Ask God to see your day and actions through His eyes
2. Thank Him
3. Review and meditate on your day and actions
4. Face your shortcomings
5. Ask God for guidance and pray about tomorrow

I'M THANKFUL FOR...

MY SINS & SHORTCOMINGS TODAY

Day 22

Morning Prayer

O Jesus, through the Immaculate Heart of Mary, I offer You my prayers, works, joys and sufferings of this day for all the intentions of Your Sacred Heart, in union with the Holy Sacrifice of the Mass throughout the world, in reparation for my sins, for the intentions of all my relatives and friends, and in particular for the intentions of the Holy Father. Amen.

Lectio Devina

READ & WRITE IT: BIBLE VERSE

REFLECT: WHAT DOES THIS MEAN TO ME?

RESPOND: WHAT DO I SAY TO GOD ABOUT THIS?

REST IN MEDITATION: HOW IS GOD ASKING ME TO CHANGE?

Examen

1. Ask God to see your day and actions through His eyes
2. Thank Him
3. Review and meditate on your day and actions
4. Face your shortcomings
5. Ask God for guidance and pray about tomorrow

I'M THANKFUL FOR...

MY SINS & SHORTCOMINGS TODAY

Day 23

O Jesus, through the Immaculate Heart of Mary, I offer You my prayers, works, joys and sufferings of this day for all the intentions of Your Sacred Heart, in union with the Holy Sacrifice of the Mass throughout the world, in reparation for my sins, for the intentions of all my relatives and friends, and in particular for the intentions of the Holy Father. Amen.

Lectio Devina

READ & WRITE IT OUT: BIBLE VERSE

REFLECT: WHAT DOES THIS MEAN TO ME?

RESPOND: WHAT DO I SAY TO GOD ABOUT THIS?

REST IN MEDITATION: HOW IS GOD ASKING ME TO CHANGE?

Examen

1. Ask God to see your day and actions through His eyes	I'M THANKFUL FOR...	MY SINS & SHORTCOMINGS TODAY
2. Thank Him		
3. Review and meditate on your day and actions		
4. Face your shortcomings		
5. Ask God for guidance and pray about tomorrow		

Day 24

Morning Prayer

O Jesus, through the Immaculate Heart of Mary, I offer You my prayers, works, joys and sufferings of this day for all the intentions of Your Sacred Heart, in union with the Holy Sacrifice of the Mass throughout the world, in reparation for my sins, for the intentions of all my relatives and friends, and in particular for the intentions of the Holy Father. Amen.

Lec-io Devina

READ & WRITE IT: BIBLE VERSE

REFLECT: WHAT DOES THIS MEAN TO ME?

RESPOND: WHAT DO I SAY TO GOD ABOUT THIS?

REST IN MEDITATION: HOW IS GOD ASKING ME TO CHANGE?

Examen

1. Ask God to see your day and actions through His eyes	I'M THANKFUL FOR...	MY SINS & SHORTCOMINGS TODAY
2. Thank Him		
3. Review and meditate on your day and actions		
4. Face your shortcomings		
5. Ask God for guidance and pray about tomorrow		

Day 25

O Jesus, through the Immaculate Heart of Mary, I offer You my prayers, works, joys and sufferings of this day for all the intentions of Your Sacred Heart, in union with the Holy Sacrifice of the Mass throughout the world, in reparation for my sins, for the intentions of all my relatives and friends, and in particular for the intentions of the Holy Father. Amen.

Lectio Devina

READ & WRITE IT OUT: BIBLE VERSE

REFLECT: WHAT DOES THIS MEAN TO ME?

RESPOND: WHAT DO I SAY TO GOD ABOUT THIS?

REST IN MEDITATION: HOW IS GOD ASKING ME TO CHANGE?

Examen

1. Ask God to see your day and actions through His eyes
2. Thank Him
3. Review and meditate on your day and actions
4. Face your shortcomings
5. Ask God for guidance and pray about tomorrow

I'M THANKFUL FOR...

MY SINS & SHORTCOMINGS TODAY

Day 26

Morning Prayer

O Jesus, through the Immaculate Heart of Mary, I offer You my prayers, works, joys and sufferings of this day for all the intentions of Your Sacred Heart, in union with the Holy Sacrifice of the Mass throughout the world, in reparation for my sins, for the intentions of all my relatives and friends, and in particular for the intentions of the Holy Father. Amen.

Lectio Devina

READ & WRITE IT: BIBLE VERSE

REFLECT: WHAT DOES THIS MEAN TO ME?

RESPOND: WHAT DO I SAY TO GOD ABOUT THIS?

REST IN MEDITATION: HOW IS GOD ASKING ME TO CHANGE?

Examen

1. Ask God to see your day and actions through His eyes
2. Thank Him
3. Review and meditate on your day and actions
4. Face your shortcomings
5. Ask God for guidance and pray about tomorrow

I'M THANKFUL FOR...

MY SINS & SHORTCOMINGS TODAY

Day 27

Morning Prayer

O Jesus, through the Immaculate Heart of Mary, I offer You my prayers, works, joys and sufferings of this day for all the intentions of Your Sacred Heart, in union with the Holy Sacrifice of the Mass throughout the world, in reparation for my sins, for the intentions of all my relatives and friends, and in particular for the intentions of the Holy Father. Amen.

Lectio Devina

READ & WRITE IT OUT: BIBLE VERSE

REFLECT: WHAT DOES THIS MEAN TO ME?

RESPOND: WHAT DO I SAY TO GOD ABOUT THIS?

REST IN MEDITATION: HOW IS GOD ASKING ME TO CHANGE?

Examen

1. Ask God to see your day and actions through His eyes
2. Thank Him
3. Review and meditate on your day and actions
4. Face your shortcomings
5. Ask God for guidance and pray about tomorrow

I'M THANKFUL FOR...

MY SINS & SHORTCOMINGS TODAY

Day 28

Morning Prayer

O Jesus, through the Immaculate Heart of Mary, I offer You my prayers, works, joys and sufferings of this day for all the intentions of Your Sacred Heart, in union with the Holy Sacrifice of the Mass throughout the world, in reparation for my sins, for the intentions of all my relatives and friends, and in particular for the intentions of the Holy Father. Amen.

Lectio Devina

READ & WRITE IT: BIBLE VERSE

REFLECT: WHAT DOES THIS MEAN TO ME?

RESPOND: WHAT DO I SAY TO GOD ABOUT THIS?

REST IN MEDITATION: HOW IS GOD ASKING ME TO CHANGE?

Examen

1. Ask God to see your day and actions through His eyes
2. Thank Him
3. Review and meditate on your day and actions
4. Face your shortcomings
5. Ask God for guidance and pray about tomorrow

I'M THANKFUL FOR...

MY SINS & SHORTCOMINGS TODAY

Day 29   *Morning Prayer*

O Jesus, through the Immaculate Heart of Mary, I offer You my prayers, works, joys and sufferings of this day for all the intentions of Your Sacred Heart, in union with the Holy Sacrifice of the Mass throughout the world, in reparation for my sins, for the intentions of all my relatives and friends, and in particular for the intentions of the Holy Father. Amen.

Lectio Devina

READ & WRITE IT OUT: BIBLE VERSE

REFLECT: WHAT DOES THIS MEAN TO ME?

RESPOND: WHAT DO I SAY TO GOD ABOUT THIS?

REST IN MEDITATION: HOW IS GOD ASKING ME TO CHANGE?

Examen

1. Ask God to see your day and actions through His eyes
2. Thank Him
3. Review and meditate on your day and actions
4. Face your shortcomings
5. Ask God for guidance and pray about tomorrow

I'M THANKFUL FOR...

MY SINS & SHORTCOMINGS TODAY

Day 30   *Morning Prayer*

O Jesus, through the Immaculate Heart of Mary, I offer You my prayers, works, joys and sufferings of this day for all the intentions of Your Sacred Heart, in union with the Holy Sacrifice of the Mass throughout the world, in reparation for my sins, for the intentions of all my relatives and friends, and in particular for the intentions of the Holy Father. Amen.

Lectio Devina

READ & WRITE IT: BIBLE VERSE

REFLECT: WHAT DOES THIS MEAN TO ME?

RESPOND: WHAT DO I SAY TO GOD ABOUT THIS?

REST IN MEDITATION: HOW IS GOD ASKING ME TO CHANGE?

Examen

1. Ask God to see your day and actions through His eyes
2. Thank Him
3. Review and meditate on your day and actions
4. Face your shortcomings
5. Ask God for guidance and pray about tomorrow

I'M THANKFUL FOR...

MY SINS & SHORTCOMINGS TODAY

PRAYERS & REFLECTIONS ON YOUR SPIRITUAL JOURNEY THIS MONTH

Jesus, I trust in You!

July

"O Jesus, when I consider the great price of Your Blood, I rejoice at its immensity, for one drop alone would have been enough for the salvation of all sinners" -St. Faustina (Diary 72)

PERSONAL RESOLUTIONS

SPIRITUAL READING LOG

LAST CONFESSION DATE

HOLY ACTIVITIES WITH MY FAMILY/ FRIENDS

PRAYER REQUESTS

✔ ROSARY & CHAPLET TRACKER

"We are all called to be great saints; don't miss the opportunity!" - Mother Angelica

Day 1

Morning Prayer

O Jesus, through the Immaculate Heart of Mary, I offer You my prayers, works, joys and sufferings of this day for all the intentions of Your Sacred Heart, in union with the Holy Sacrifice of the Mass throughout the world, in reparation for my sins, for the intentions of all my relatives and friends, and in particular for the intentions of the Holy Father. Amen.

Lectio Devina

READ & WRITE IT OUT: BIBLE VERSE

REFLECT: WHAT DOES THIS MEAN TO ME?

RESPOND: WHAT DO I SAY TO GOD ABOUT THIS?

REST IN MEDITATION: HOW IS GOD ASKING ME TO CHANGE?

Examen

1. Ask God to see your day and actions through His eyes
2. Thank Him
3. Review and meditate on your day and actions
4. Face your shortcomings
5. Ask God for guidance and pray about tomorrow

I'M THANKFUL FOR...

MY SINS & SHORTCOMINGS TODAY

Day 2

Morning Prayer

O Jesus, through the Immaculate Heart of Mary, I offer You my prayers, works, joys and sufferings of this day for all the intentions of Your Sacred Heart, in union with the Holy Sacrifice of the Mass throughout the world, in reparation for my sins, for the intentions of all my relatives and friends, and in particular for the intentions of the Holy Father. Amen.

Lectio Devina

READ & WRITE IT: BIBLE VERSE

REFLECT: WHAT DOES THIS MEAN TO ME?

RESPOND: WHAT DO I SAY TO GOD ABOUT THIS?

REST IN MEDITATION: HOW IS GOD ASKING ME TO CHANGE?

Examen

1. Ask God to see your day and actions through His eyes
2. Thank Him
3. Review and meditate on your day and actions
4. Face your shortcomings
5. Ask God for guidance and pray about tomorrow

I'M THANKFUL FOR...

MY SINS & SHORTCOMINGS TODAY

Day 3

Morning Prayer

O Jesus, through the Immaculate Heart of Mary, I offer You my prayers, works, joys and sufferings of this day for all the intentions of Your Sacred Heart, in union with the Holy Sacrifice of the Mass throughout the world, in reparation for my sins, for the intentions of all my relatives and friends, and in particular for the intentions of the Holy Father. Amen.

Lectio Devina

READ & WRITE IT OUT: BIBLE VERSE

REFLECT: WHAT DOES THIS MEAN TO ME?

RESPOND: WHAT DO I SAY TO GOD ABOUT THIS?

REST IN MEDITATION: HOW IS GOD ASKING ME TO CHANGE?

Examen

1. Ask God to see your day and actions through His eyes
2. Thank Him
3. Review and meditate on your day and actions
4. Face your shortcomings
5. Ask God for guidance and pray about tomorrow

I'M THANKFUL FOR...

MY SINS & SHORTCOMINGS TODAY

Day 4

Morning Prayer

O Jesus, through the Immaculate Heart of Mary, I offer You my prayers, works, joys and sufferings of this day for all the intentions of Your Sacred Heart, in union with the Holy Sacrifice of the Mass throughout the world, in reparation for my sins, for the intentions of all my relatives and friends, and in particular for the intentions of the Holy Father. Amen.

Lectio Devina

READ & WRITE IT: BIBLE VERSE

REFLECT: WHAT DOES THIS MEAN TO ME?

RESPOND: WHAT DO I SAY TO GOD ABOUT THIS?

REST IN MEDITATION: HOW IS GOD ASKING ME TO CHANGE?

Examen

1. Ask God to see your day and actions through His eyes
2. Thank Him
3. Review and meditate on your day and actions
4. Face your shortcomings
5. Ask God for guidance and pray about tomorrow

I'M THANKFUL FOR...

MY SINS & SHORTCOMINGS TODAY

Day 5

Morning Prayer

O Jesus, through the Immaculate Heart of Mary, I offer You my prayers, works, joys and sufferings of this day for all the intentions of Your Sacred Heart, in union with the Holy Sacrifice of the Mass throughout the world, in reparation for my sins, for the intentions of all my relatives and friends, and in particular for the intentions of the Holy Father. Amen.

Lectio Devina

READ & WRITE IT OUT: BIBLE VERSE

REFLECT: WHAT DOES THIS MEAN TO ME?

RESPOND: WHAT DO I SAY TO GOD ABOUT THIS?

REST IN MEDITATION: HOW IS GOD ASKING ME TO CHANGE?

Examen

1. Ask God to see your day and actions through His eyes
2. Thank Him
3. Review and meditate on your day and actions
4. Face your shortcomings
5. Ask God for guidance and pray about tomorrow

I'M THANKFUL FOR...

MY SINS & SHORTCOMINGS TODAY

Day 6

Morning Prayer

O Jesus, through the Immaculate Heart of Mary, I offer You my prayers, works, joys and sufferings of this day for all the intentions of Your Sacred Heart, in union with the Holy Sacrifice of the Mass throughout the world, in reparation for my sins, for the intentions of all my relatives and friends, and in particular for the intentions of the Holy Father. Amen.

Lec~io Devina

READ & WRITE IT: BIBLE VERSE

REFLECT: WHAT DOES THIS MEAN TO ME?

RESPOND: WHAT DO I SAY TO GOD ABOUT THIS?

REST IN MEDITATION: HOW IS GOD ASKING ME TO CHANGE?

Examen

1. Ask God to see your day and actions through His eyes
2. Thank Him
3. Review and meditate on your day and actions
4. Face your shortcomings
5. Ask God for guidance and pray about tomorrow

I'M THANKFUL FOR...

MY SINS & SHORTCOMINGS TODAY

Day 7   *Morning Prayer*

O Jesus, through the Immaculate Heart of Mary, I offer You my prayers, works, joys and sufferings of this day for all the intentions of Your Sacred Heart, in union with the Holy Sacrifice of the Mass throughout the world, in reparation for my sins, for the intentions of all my relatives and friends, and in particular for the intentions of the Holy Father. Amen.

READ & WRITE IT OUT: BIBLE VERSE

REFLECT: WHAT DOES THIS MEAN TO ME?

RESPOND: WHAT DO I SAY TO GOD ABOUT THIS?

REST IN MEDITATION: HOW IS GOD ASKING ME TO CHANGE?

1. Ask God to see your day and actions through His eyes
2. Thank Him
3. Review and meditate on your day and actions
4. Face your shortcomings
5. Ask God for guidance and pray about tomorrow

I'M THANKFUL FOR...   MY SINS & SHORTCOMINGS TODAY

Day 8   *Morning Prayer*

O Jesus, through the Immaculate Heart of Mary, I offer You my prayers, works, joys and sufferings of this day for all the intentions of Your Sacred Heart, in union with the Holy Sacrifice of the Mass throughout the world, in reparation for my sins, for the intentions of all my relatives and friends, and in particular for the intentions of the Holy Father. Amen.

READ & WRITE IT: BIBLE VERSE

REFLECT: WHAT DOES THIS MEAN TO ME?

RESPOND: WHAT DO I SAY TO GOD ABOUT THIS?

REST IN MEDITATION: HOW IS GOD ASKING ME TO CHANGE?

1. Ask God to see your day and actions through His eyes
2. Thank Him
3. Review and meditate on your day and actions
4. Face your shortcomings
5. Ask God for guidance and pray about tomorrow

I'M THANKFUL FOR...   MY SINS & SHORTCOMINGS TODAY

Day 9   *Morning Prayer*

O Jesus, through the Immaculate Heart of Mary, I offer You my prayers, works, joys and sufferings of this day for all the intentions of Your Sacred Heart, in union with the Holy Sacrifice of the Mass throughout the world, in reparation for my sins, for the intentions of all my relatives and friends, and in particular for the intentions of the Holy Father. Amen.

Lectio Devina

READ & WRITE IT OUT: BIBLE VERSE

REFLECT: WHAT DOES THIS MEAN TO ME?

RESPOND: WHAT DO I SAY TO GOD ABOUT THIS?

REST IN MEDITATION: HOW IS GOD ASKING ME TO CHANGE?

Examen

1. Ask God to see your day and actions through His eyes
2. Thank Him
3. Review and meditate on your day and actions
4. Face your shortcomings
5. Ask God for guidance and pray about tomorrow

I'M THANKFUL FOR...

MY SINS & SHORTCOMINGS TODAY

Day 10   *Morning Prayer*

O Jesus, through the Immaculate Heart of Mary, I offer You my prayers, works, joys and sufferings of this day for all the intentions of Your Sacred Heart, in union with the Holy Sacrifice of the Mass throughout the world, in reparation for my sins, for the intentions of all my relatives and friends, and in particular for the intentions of the Holy Father. Amen.

Lectio Devina

READ & WRITE IT: BIBLE VERSE

REFLECT: WHAT DOES THIS MEAN TO ME?

RESPOND: WHAT DO I SAY TO GOD ABOUT THIS?

REST IN MEDITATION: HOW IS GOD ASKING ME TO CHANGE?

Examen

1. Ask God to see your day and actions through His eyes
2. Thank Him
3. Review and meditate on your day and actions
4. Face your shortcomings
5. Ask God for guidance and pray about tomorrow

I'M THANKFUL FOR...

MY SINS & SHORTCOMINGS TODAY

Day 11

O Jesus, through the Immaculate Heart of Mary, I offer You my prayers, works, joys and sufferings of this day for all the intentions of Your Sacred Heart, in union with the Holy Sacrifice of the Mass throughout the world, in reparation for my sins, for the intentions of all my relatives and friends, and in particular for the intentions of the Holy Father. Amen.

Lectio Devina

READ & WRITE IT OUT: BIBLE VERSE

REFLECT: WHAT DOES THIS MEAN TO ME?

RESPOND: WHAT DO I SAY TO GOD ABOUT THIS?

REST IN MEDITATION: HOW IS GOD ASKING ME TO CHANGE?

Examen

1. Ask God to see your day and actions through His eyes
2. Thank Him
3. Review and meditate on your day and actions
4. Face your shortcomings
5. Ask God for guidance and pray about tomorrow

I'M THANKFUL FOR...

MY SINS & SHORTCOMINGS TODAY

Day 12

Morning Prayer

O Jesus, through the Immaculate Heart of Mary, I offer You my prayers, works, joys and sufferings of this day for all the intentions of Your Sacred Heart, in union with the Holy Sacrifice of the Mass throughout the world, in reparation for my sins, for the intentions of all my relatives and friends, and in particular for the intentions of the Holy Father. Amen.

Lectio Devina

READ & WRITE IT: BIBLE VERSE

REFLECT: WHAT DOES THIS MEAN TO ME?

RESPOND: WHAT DO I SAY TO GOD ABOUT THIS?

REST IN MEDITATION: HOW IS GOD ASKING ME TO CHANGE?

Examen

1. Ask God to see your day and actions through His eyes
2. Thank Him
3. Review and meditate on your day and actions
4. Face your shortcomings
5. Ask God for guidance and pray about tomorrow

I'M THANKFUL FOR...

MY SINS & SHORTCOMINGS TODAY

Day 13   *Morning Prayer*

O Jesus, through the Immaculate Heart of Mary, I offer You my prayers, works, joys and sufferings of this day for all the intentions of Your Sacred Heart, in union with the Holy Sacrifice of the Mass throughout the world, in reparation for my sins, for the intentions of all my relatives and friends, and in particular for the intentions of the Holy Father. Amen.

Lectio Devina

READ & WRITE IT OUT: BIBLE VERSE

REFLECT: WHAT DOES THIS MEAN TO ME?

RESPOND: WHAT DO I SAY TO GOD ABOUT THIS?

REST IN MEDITATION: HOW IS GOD ASKING ME TO CHANGE?

Examen

1. Ask God to see your day and actions through His eyes
2. Thank Him
3. Review and meditate on your day and actions
4. Face your shortcomings
5. Ask God for guidance and pray about tomorrow

I'M THANKFUL FOR...

MY SINS & SHORTCOMINGS TODAY

Day 14   *Morning Prayer*

O Jesus, through the Immaculate Heart of Mary, I offer You my prayers, works, joys and sufferings of this day for all the intentions of Your Sacred Heart, in union with the Holy Sacrifice of the Mass throughout the world, in reparation for my sins, for the intentions of all my relatives and friends, and in particular for the intentions of the Holy Father. Amen.

Lectio Devina

READ & WRITE IT: BIBLE VERSE

REFLECT: WHAT DOES THIS MEAN TO ME?

RESPOND: WHAT DO I SAY TO GOD ABOUT THIS?

REST IN MEDITATION: HOW IS GOD ASKING ME TO CHANGE?

Examen

1. Ask God to see your day and actions through His eyes
2. Thank Him
3. Review and meditate on your day and actions
4. Face your shortcomings
5. Ask God for guidance and pray about tomorrow

I'M THANKFUL FOR...

MY SINS & SHORTCOMINGS TODAY

Day 15

O Jesus, through the Immaculate Heart of Mary, I offer You my prayers, works, joys and sufferings of this day for all the intentions of Your Sacred Heart, in union with the Holy Sacrifice of the Mass throughout the world, in reparation for my sins, for the intentions of all my relatives and friends, and in particular for the intentions of the Holy Father. Amen.

READ & WRITE IT OUT: BIBLE VERSE

REFLECT: WHAT DOES THIS MEAN TO ME?

RESPOND: WHAT DO I SAY TO GOD ABOUT THIS?

REST IN MEDITATION: HOW IS GOD ASKING ME TO CHANGE?

Lectio Devina

1. Ask God to see your day and actions through His eyes	I'M THANKFUL FOR...	MY SINS & SHORTCOMINGS TODAY
2. Thank Him		
3. Review and meditate on your day and actions		
4. Face your shortcomings		
5. Ask God for guidance and pray about tomorrow		

Examen

Day 16

Morning Prayer

O Jesus, through the Immaculate Heart of Mary, I offer You my prayers, works, joys and sufferings of this day for all the intentions of Your Sacred Heart, in union with the Holy Sacrifice of the Mass throughout the world, in reparation for my sins, for the intentions of all my relatives and friends, and in particular for the intentions of the Holy Father. Amen.

READ & WRITE IT: BIBLE VERSE

REFLECT: WHAT DOES THIS MEAN TO ME?

RESPOND: WHAT DO I SAY TO GOD ABOUT THIS?

REST IN MEDITATION: HOW IS GOD ASKING ME TO CHANGE?

Lectio Devina

1. Ask God to see your day and actions through His eyes	I'M THANKFUL FOR...	MY SINS & SHORTCOMINGS TODAY
2. Thank Him		
3. Review and meditate on your day and actions		
4. Face your shortcomings		
5. Ask God for guidance and pray about tomorrow		

Examen

Day 17   *Morning Prayer*

O Jesus, through the Immaculate Heart of Mary, I offer You my prayers, works, joys and sufferings of this day for all the intentions of Your Sacred Heart, in union with the Holy Sacrifice of the Mass throughout the world, in reparation for my sins, for the intentions of all my relatives and friends, and in particular for the intentions of the Holy Father. Amen.

Lectio Devina

READ & WRITE IT OUT: BIBLE VERSE

REFLECT: WHAT DOES THIS MEAN TO ME?

RESPOND: WHAT DO I SAY TO GOD ABOUT THIS?

REST IN MEDITATION: HOW IS GOD ASKING ME TO CHANGE?

Examen

1. Ask God to see your day and actions through His eyes
2. Thank Him
3. Review and meditate on your day and actions
4. Face your shortcomings
5. Ask God for guidance and pray about tomorrow

I'M THANKFUL FOR...   MY SINS & SHORTCOMINGS TODAY

Day 18   *Morning Prayer*

O Jesus, through the Immaculate Heart of Mary, I offer You my prayers, works, joys and sufferings of this day for all the intentions of Your Sacred Heart, in union with the Holy Sacrifice of the Mass throughout the world, in reparation for my sins, for the intentions of all my relatives and friends, and in particular for the intentions of the Holy Father. Amen.

Lectio Devina

READ & WRITE IT: BIBLE VERSE

REFLECT: WHAT DOES THIS MEAN TO ME?

RESPOND: WHAT DO I SAY TO GOD ABOUT THIS?

REST IN MEDITATION: HOW IS GOD ASKING ME TO CHANGE?

Examen

1. Ask God to see your day and actions through His eyes
2. Thank Him
3. Review and meditate on your day and actions
4. Face your shortcomings
5. Ask God for guidance and pray about tomorrow

I'M THANKFUL FOR...   MY SINS & SHORTCOMINGS TODAY

Day 19

O Jesus, through the Immaculate Heart of Mary, I offer You my prayers, works, joys and sufferings of this day for all the intentions of Your Sacred Heart, in union with the Holy Sacrifice of the Mass throughout the world, in reparation for my sins, for the intentions of all my relatives and friends, and in particular for the intentions of the Holy Father. Amen.

Lectio Devina

READ & WRITE IT OUT: BIBLE VERSE

REFLECT: WHAT DOES THIS MEAN TO ME?

RESPOND: WHAT DO I SAY TO GOD ABOUT THIS?

REST IN MEDITATION: HOW IS GOD ASKING ME TO CHANGE?

Examen

1. Ask God to see your day and actions through His eyes
2. Thank Him
3. Review and meditate on your day and actions
4. Face your shortcomings
5. Ask God for guidance and pray about tomorrow

I'M THANKFUL FOR...

MY SINS & SHORTCOMINGS TODAY

Day 20

Morning Prayer

O Jesus, through the Immaculate Heart of Mary, I offer You my prayers, works, joys and sufferings of this day for all the intentions of Your Sacred Heart, in union with the Holy Sacrifice of the Mass throughout the world, in reparation for my sins, for the intentions of all my relatives and friends, and in particular for the intentions of the Holy Father. Amen.

Lectio Devina

READ & WRITE IT: BIBLE VERSE

REFLECT: WHAT DOES THIS MEAN TO ME?

RESPOND: WHAT DO I SAY TO GOD ABOUT THIS?

REST IN MEDITATION: HOW IS GOD ASKING ME TO CHANGE?

Examen

1. Ask God to see your day and actions through His eyes
2. Thank Him
3. Review and meditate on your day and actions
4. Face your shortcomings
5. Ask God for guidance and pray about tomorrow

I'M THANKFUL FOR...

MY SINS & SHORTCOMINGS TODAY

Day 21   *Morning Prayer*

O Jesus, through the Immaculate Heart of Mary, I offer You my prayers, works, joys and sufferings of this day for all the intentions of Your Sacred Heart, in union with the Holy Sacrifice of the Mass throughout the world, in reparation for my sins, for the intentions of all my relatives and friends, and in particular for the intentions of the Holy Father. Amen.

Lectio Devina

READ & WRITE IT OUT: BIBLE VERSE

REFLECT: WHAT DOES THIS MEAN TO ME?

RESPOND: WHAT DO I SAY TO GOD ABOUT THIS?

REST IN MEDITATION: HOW IS GOD ASKING ME TO CHANGE?

Examen

1. Ask God to see your day and actions through His eyes
2. Thank Him
3. Review and meditate on your day and actions
4. Face your shortcomings
5. Ask God for guidance and pray about tomorrow

I'M THANKFUL FOR...

MY SINS & SHORTCOMINGS TODAY

Day 22   *Morning Prayer*

O Jesus, through the Immaculate Heart of Mary, I offer You my prayers, works, joys and sufferings of this day for all the intentions of Your Sacred Heart, in union with the Holy Sacrifice of the Mass throughout the world, in reparation for my sins, for the intentions of all my relatives and friends, and in particular for the intentions of the Holy Father. Amen.

Lectio Devina

READ & WRITE IT: BIBLE VERSE

REFLECT: WHAT DOES THIS MEAN TO ME?

RESPOND: WHAT DO I SAY TO GOD ABOUT THIS?

REST IN MEDITATION: HOW IS GOD ASKING ME TO CHANGE?

Examen

1. Ask God to see your day and actions through His eyes
2. Thank Him
3. Review and meditate on your day and actions
4. Face your shortcomings
5. Ask God for guidance and pray about tomorrow

I'M THANKFUL FOR...

MY SINS & SHORTCOMINGS TODAY

Day 23   *Morning Prayer*

O Jesus, through the Immaculate Heart of Mary, I offer You my prayers, works, joys and sufferings of this day for all the intentions of Your Sacred Heart, in union with the Holy Sacrifice of the Mass throughout the world, in reparation for my sins, for the intentions of all my relatives and friends, and in particular for the intentions of the Holy Father. Amen.

READ & WRITE IT OUT: BIBLE VERSE

REFLECT: WHAT DOES THIS MEAN TO ME?

RESPOND: WHAT DO I SAY TO GOD ABOUT THIS?

REST IN MEDITATION: HOW IS GOD ASKING ME TO CHANGE?

1. Ask God to see your day and actions through His eyes
2. Thank Him
3. Review and meditate on your day and actions
4. Face your shortcomings
5. Ask God for guidance and pray about tomorrow

I'M THANKFUL FOR...

MY SINS & SHORTCOMINGS TODAY

Day 24   *Morning Prayer*

O Jesus, through the Immaculate Heart of Mary, I offer You my prayers, works, joys and sufferings of this day for all the intentions of Your Sacred Heart, in union with the Holy Sacrifice of the Mass throughout the world, in reparation for my sins, for the intentions of all my relatives and friends, and in particular for the intentions of the Holy Father. Amen.

READ & WRITE IT: BIBLE VERSE

REFLECT: WHAT DOES THIS MEAN TO ME?

RESPOND: WHAT DO I SAY TO GOD ABOUT THIS?

REST IN MEDITATION: HOW IS GOD ASKING ME TO CHANGE?

1. Ask God to see your day and actions through His eyes
2. Thank Him
3. Review and meditate on your day and actions
4. Face your shortcomings
5. Ask God for guidance and pray about tomorrow

I'M THANKFUL FOR...

MY SINS & SHORTCOMINGS TODAY

Day 25

Morning Prayer

O Jesus, through the Immaculate Heart of Mary, I offer You my prayers, works, joys and sufferings of this day for all the intentions of Your Sacred Heart, in union with the Holy Sacrifice of the Mass throughout the world, in reparation for my sins, for the intentions of all my relatives and friends, and in particular for the intentions of the Holy Father. Amen.

Lectio Devina

READ & WRITE IT OUT: BIBLE VERSE

REFLECT: WHAT DOES THIS MEAN TO ME?

RESPOND: WHAT DO I SAY TO GOD ABOUT THIS?

REST IN MEDITATION: HOW IS GOD ASKING ME TO CHANGE?

Examen

1. Ask God to see your day and actions through His eyes
2. Thank Him
3. Review and meditate on your day and actions
4. Face your shortcomings
5. Ask God for guidance and pray about tomorrow

I'M THANKFUL FOR...

MY SINS & SHORTCOMINGS TODAY

Day 26

Morning Prayer

O Jesus, through the Immaculate Heart of Mary, I offer You my prayers, works, joys and sufferings of this day for all the intentions of Your Sacred Heart, in union with the Holy Sacrifice of the Mass throughout the world, in reparation for my sins, for the intentions of all my relatives and friends, and in particular for the intentions of the Holy Father. Amen.

Lec-io Devina

READ & WRITE IT: BIBLE VERSE

REFLECT: WHAT DOES THIS MEAN TO ME?

RESPOND: WHAT DO I SAY TO GOD ABOUT THIS?

REST IN MEDITATION: HOW IS GOD ASKING ME TO CHANGE?

Examen

1. Ask God to see your day and actions through His eyes
2. Thank Him
3. Review and meditate on your day and actions
4. Face your shortcomings
5. Ask God for guidance and pray about tomorrow

I'M THANKFUL FOR...

MY SINS & SHORTCOMINGS TODAY

Day 27

Morning Prayer

O Jesus, through the Immaculate Heart of Mary, I offer You my prayers, works, joys and sufferings of this day for all the intentions of Your Sacred Heart, in union with the Holy Sacrifice of the Mass throughout the world, in reparation for my sins, for the intentions of all my relatives and friends, and in particular for the intentions of the Holy Father. Amen.

Lectio Devina

READ & WRITE IT OUT: BIBLE VERSE

REFLECT: WHAT DOES THIS MEAN TO ME?

RESPOND: WHAT DO I SAY TO GOD ABOUT THIS?

REST IN MEDITATION: HOW IS GOD ASKING ME TO CHANGE?

Examen

1. Ask God to see your day and actions through His eyes
2. Thank Him
3. Review and meditate on your day and actions
4. Face your shortcomings
5. Ask God for guidance and pray about tomorrow

I'M THANKFUL FOR...

MY SINS & SHORTCOMINGS TODAY

Day 28

Morning Prayer

O Jesus, through the Immaculate Heart of Mary, I offer You my prayers, works, joys and sufferings of this day for all the intentions of Your Sacred Heart, in union with the Holy Sacrifice of the Mass throughout the world, in reparation for my sins, for the intentions of all my relatives and friends, and in particular for the intentions of the Holy Father. Amen.

Lectio Devina

READ & WRITE IT: BIBLE VERSE

REFLECT: WHAT DOES THIS MEAN TO ME?

RESPOND: WHAT DO I SAY TO GOD ABOUT THIS?

REST IN MEDITATION: HOW IS GOD ASKING ME TO CHANGE?

Examen

1. Ask God to see your day and actions through His eyes
2. Thank Him
3. Review and meditate on your day and actions
4. Face your shortcomings
5. Ask God for guidance and pray about tomorrow

I'M THANKFUL FOR...

MY SINS & SHORTCOMINGS TODAY

Day 29

O Jesus, through the Immaculate Heart of Mary, I offer You my prayers, works, joys and sufferings of this day for all the intentions of Your Sacred Heart, in union with the Holy Sacrifice of the Mass throughout the world, in reparation for my sins, for the intentions of all my relatives and friends, and in particular for the intentions of the Holy Father. Amen.

Lectio Devina

READ & WRITE IT OUT: BIBLE VERSE

REFLECT: WHAT DOES THIS MEAN TO ME?

RESPOND: WHAT DO I SAY TO GOD ABOUT THIS?

REST IN MEDITATION: HOW IS GOD ASKING ME TO CHANGE?

Examen

1. Ask God to see your day and actions through His eyes
2. Thank Him
3. Review and meditate on your day and actions
4. Face your shortcomings
5. Ask God for guidance and pray about tomorrow

I'M THANKFUL FOR...

MY SINS & SHORTCOMINGS TODAY

Day 30

Morning Prayer

O Jesus, through the Immaculate Heart of Mary, I offer You my prayers, works, joys and sufferings of this day for all the intentions of Your Sacred Heart, in union with the Holy Sacrifice of the Mass throughout the world, in reparation for my sins, for the intentions of all my relatives and friends, and in particular for the intentions of the Holy Father. Amen.

Lectio Devina

READ & WRITE IT: BIBLE VERSE

REFLECT: WHAT DOES THIS MEAN TO ME?

RESPOND: WHAT DO I SAY TO GOD ABOUT THIS?

REST IN MEDITATION: HOW IS GOD ASKING ME TO CHANGE?

Examen

1. Ask God to see your day and actions through His eyes
2. Thank Him
3. Review and meditate on your day and actions
4. Face your shortcomings
5. Ask God for guidance and pray about tomorrow

I'M THANKFUL FOR...

MY SINS & SHORTCOMINGS TODAY

Day 31

O Jesus, through the Immaculate Heart of Mary, I offer You my prayers, works, joys and sufferings of this day for all the intentions of Your Sacred Heart, in union with the Holy Sacrifice of the Mass throughout the world, in reparation for my sins, for the intentions of all my relatives and friends, and in particular for the intentions of the Holy Father. Amen.

Lectio Devina

READ & WRITE IT OUT: BIBLE VERSE

REFLECT: WHAT DOES THIS MEAN TO ME?

RESPOND: WHAT DO I SAY TO GOD ABOUT THIS?

REST IN MEDITATION: HOW IS GOD ASKING ME TO CHANGE?

Examen

1. Ask God to see your day and actions through His eyes
2. Thank Him
3. Review and meditate on your day and actions
4. Face your shortcomings
5. Ask God for guidance and pray about tomorrow

I'M THANKFUL FOR...

MY SINS & SHORTCOMINGS TODAY

PRAYERS & REFLECTIONS ON YOUR SPIRITUAL JOURNEY THIS MONTH

August

"Mary, give me your heart: so beautiful, so pure, so immaculate; your heart so full of love and humility that I may receive Jesus in the Bread of Life and love Him as you love Him."
-St. Teresa of Calcutta

PERSONAL RESOLUTIONS

SPIRITUAL READING LOG

LAST CONFESSION DATE

HOLY ACTIVITIES WITH MY FAMILY/ FRIENDS

PRAYER REQUESTS

✔ ROSARY & CHAPLET TRACKER

"We are all called to be great saints; don't miss the opportunity!" - Mother Angelica

Day 1

Morning Prayer

O Jesus, through the Immaculate Heart of Mary, I offer You my prayers, works, joys and sufferings of this day for all the intentions of Your Sacred Heart, in union with the Holy Sacrifice of the Mass throughout the world, in reparation for my sins, for the intentions of all my relatives and friends, and in particular for the intentions of the Holy Father. Amen.

Lectio Devina

READ & WRITE IT OUT: BIBLE VERSE

REFLECT: WHAT DOES THIS MEAN TO ME?

RESPOND: WHAT DO I SAY TO GOD ABOUT THIS?

REST IN MEDITATION: HOW IS GOD ASKING ME TO CHANGE?

Examen

1. Ask God to see your day and actions through His eyes
2. Thank Him
3. Review and meditate on your day and actions
4. Face your shortcomings
5. Ask God for guidance and pray about tomorrow

I'M THANKFUL FOR...

MY SINS & SHORTCOMINGS TODAY

Day 2

Morning Prayer

O Jesus, through the Immaculate Heart of Mary, I offer You my prayers, works, joys and sufferings of this day for all the intentions of Your Sacred Heart, in union with the Holy Sacrifice of the Mass throughout the world, in reparation for my sins, for the intentions of all my relatives and friends, and in particular for the intentions of the Holy Father. Amen.

Lectio Devina

READ & WRITE IT: BIBLE VERSE

REFLECT: WHAT DOES THIS MEAN TO ME?

RESPOND: WHAT DO I SAY TO GOD ABOUT THIS?

REST IN MEDITATION: HOW IS GOD ASKING ME TO CHANGE?

Examen

1. Ask God to see your day and actions through His eyes
2. Thank Him
3. Review and meditate on your day and actions
4. Face your shortcomings
5. Ask God for guidance and pray about tomorrow

I'M THANKFUL FOR...

MY SINS & SHORTCOMINGS TODAY

Day 3   *Morning Prayer*

O Jesus, through the Immaculate Heart of Mary, I offer You my prayers, works, joys and sufferings of this day for all the intentions of Your Sacred Heart, in union with the Holy Sacrifice of the Mass throughout the world, in reparation for my sins, for the intentions of all my relatives and friends, and in particular for the intentions of the Holy Father. Amen.

READ & WRITE IT OUT: BIBLE VERSE

Lectio Devina

REFLECT: WHAT DOES THIS MEAN TO ME?

RESPOND: WHAT DO I SAY TO GOD ABOUT THIS?

REST IN MEDITATION: HOW IS GOD ASKING ME TO CHANGE?

Examen

1. Ask God to see your day and actions through His eyes
2. Thank Him
3. Review and meditate on your day and actions
4. Face your shortcomings
5. Ask God for guidance and pray about tomorrow

I'M THANKFUL FOR...   MY SINS & SHORTCOMINGS TODAY

Day 4   *Morning Prayer*

O Jesus, through the Immaculate Heart of Mary, I offer You my prayers, works, joys and sufferings of this day for all the intentions of Your Sacred Heart, in union with the Holy Sacrifice of the Mass throughout the world, in reparation for my sins, for the intentions of all my relatives and friends, and in particular for the intentions of the Holy Father. Amen.

READ & WRITE IT: BIBLE VERSE

Lectio Devina

REFLECT: WHAT DOES THIS MEAN TO ME?

RESPOND: WHAT DO I SAY TO GOD ABOUT THIS?

REST IN MEDITATION: HOW IS GOD ASKING ME TO CHANGE?

Examen

1. Ask God to see your day and actions through His eyes
2. Thank Him
3. Review and meditate on your day and actions
4. Face your shortcomings
5. Ask God for guidance and pray about tomorrow

I'M THANKFUL FOR...   MY SINS & SHORTCOMINGS TODAY

Day 5   *Morning Prayer*

O Jesus, through the Immaculate Heart of Mary, I offer You my prayers, works, joys and sufferings of this day for all the intentions of Your Sacred Heart, in union with the Holy Sacrifice of the Mass throughout the world, in reparation for my sins, for the intentions of all my relatives and friends, and in particular for the intentions of the Holy Father. Amen.

READ & WRITE IT OUT: BIBLE VERSE

REFLECT: WHAT DOES THIS MEAN TO ME?

RESPOND: WHAT DO I SAY TO GOD ABOUT THIS?

REST IN MEDITATION: HOW IS GOD ASKING ME TO CHANGE?

Lectio Devina

1. Ask God to see your day and actions through His eyes
2. Thank Him
3. Review and meditate on your day and actions
4. Face your shortcomings
5. Ask God for guidance and pray about tomorrow

I'M THANKFUL FOR...

MY SINS & SHORTCOMINGS TODAY

Examen

Day 6   *Morning Prayer*

O Jesus, through the Immaculate Heart of Mary, I offer You my prayers, works, joys and sufferings of this day for all the intentions of Your Sacred Heart, in union with the Holy Sacrifice of the Mass throughout the world, in reparation for my sins, for the intentions of all my relatives and friends, and in particular for the intentions of the Holy Father. Amen.

READ & WRITE IT: BIBLE VERSE

REFLECT: WHAT DOES THIS MEAN TO ME?

RESPOND: WHAT DO I SAY TO GOD ABOUT THIS?

REST IN MEDITATION: HOW IS GOD ASKING ME TO CHANGE?

Lectio Devina

1. Ask God to see your day and actions through His eyes
2. Thank Him
3. Review and meditate on your day and actions
4. Face your shortcomings
5. Ask God for guidance and pray about tomorrow

I'M THANKFUL FOR...

MY SINS & SHORTCOMINGS TODAY

Examen

Day 7   *Morning Prayer*

O Jesus, through the Immaculate Heart of Mary, I offer You my prayers, works, joys and sufferings of this day for all the intentions of Your Sacred Heart, in union with the Holy Sacrifice of the Mass throughout the world, in reparation for my sins, for the intentions of all my relatives and friends, and in particular for the intentions of the Holy Father. Amen.

Lectio Devina

READ & WRITE IT OUT: BIBLE VERSE

REFLECT: WHAT DOES THIS MEAN TO ME?

RESPOND: WHAT DO I SAY TO GOD ABOUT THIS?

REST IN MEDITATION: HOW IS GOD ASKING ME TO CHANGE?

Examen

1. Ask God to see your day and actions through His eyes
2. Thank Him
3. Review and meditate on your day and actions
4. Face your shortcomings
5. Ask God for guidance and pray about tomorrow

I'M THANKFUL FOR...

MY SINS & SHORTCOMINGS TODAY

Day 8   *Morning Prayer*

O Jesus, through the Immaculate Heart of Mary, I offer You my prayers, works, joys and sufferings of this day for all the intentions of Your Sacred Heart, in union with the Holy Sacrifice of the Mass throughout the world, in reparation for my sins, for the intentions of all my relatives and friends, and in particular for the intentions of the Holy Father. Amen.

Lectio Devina

READ & WRITE IT: BIBLE VERSE

REFLECT: WHAT DOES THIS MEAN TO ME?

RESPOND: WHAT DO I SAY TO GOD ABOUT THIS?

REST IN MEDITATION: HOW IS GOD ASKING ME TO CHANGE?

Examen

1. Ask God to see your day and actions through His eyes
2. Thank Him
3. Review and meditate on your day and actions
4. Face your shortcomings
5. Ask God for guidance and pray about tomorrow

I'M THANKFUL FOR...

MY SINS & SHORTCOMINGS TODAY

Day 9   *Morning Prayer*

O Jesus, through the Immaculate Heart of Mary, I offer You my prayers, works, joys and sufferings of this day for all the intentions of Your Sacred Heart, in union with the Holy Sacrifice of the Mass throughout the world, in reparation for my sins, for the intentions of all my relatives and friends, and in particular for the intentions of the Holy Father. Amen.

READ & WRITE IT OUT: BIBLE VERSE

REFLECT: WHAT DOES THIS MEAN TO ME?

RESPOND: WHAT DO I SAY TO GOD ABOUT THIS?

REST IN MEDITATION: HOW IS GOD ASKING ME TO CHANGE?

Lectio Devina

1. Ask God to see your day and actions through His eyes
2. Thank Him
3. Review and meditate on your day and actions
4. Face your shortcomings
5. Ask God for guidance and pray about tomorrow

I'M THANKFUL FOR...   MY SINS & SHORTCOMINGS TODAY

Examen

Day 10   *Morning Prayer*

O Jesus, through the Immaculate Heart of Mary, I offer You my prayers, works, joys and sufferings of this day for all the intentions of Your Sacred Heart, in union with the Holy Sacrifice of the Mass throughout the world, in reparation for my sins, for the intentions of all my relatives and friends, and in particular for the intentions of the Holy Father. Amen.

READ & WRITE IT: BIBLE VERSE

REFLECT: WHAT DOES THIS MEAN TO ME?

RESPOND: WHAT DO I SAY TO GOD ABOUT THIS?

REST IN MEDITATION: HOW IS GOD ASKING ME TO CHANGE?

Lectio Devina

1. Ask God to see your day and actions through His eyes
2. Thank Him
3. Review and meditate on your day and actions
4. Face your shortcomings
5. Ask God for guidance and pray about tomorrow

I'M THANKFUL FOR...   MY SINS & SHORTCOMINGS TODAY

Examen

Day 11   *Morning Prayer*

O Jesus, through the Immaculate Heart of Mary, I offer You my prayers, works, joys and sufferings of this day for all the intentions of Your Sacred Heart, in union with the Holy Sacrifice of the Mass throughout the world, in reparation for my sins, for the intentions of all my relatives and friends, and in particular for the intentions of the Holy Father. Amen.

READ & WRITE IT OUT: BIBLE VERSE

REFLECT: WHAT DOES THIS MEAN TO ME?

RESPOND: WHAT DO I SAY TO GOD ABOUT THIS?

REST IN MEDITATION: HOW IS GOD ASKING ME TO CHANGE?

Lectio Devina

1. Ask God to see your day and actions through His eyes
2. Thank Him
3. Review and meditate on your day and actions
4. Face your shortcomings
5. Ask God for guidance and pray about tomorrow

I'M THANKFUL FOR...   MY SINS & SHORTCOMINGS TODAY

Examen

Day 12   *Morning Prayer*

O Jesus, through the Immaculate Heart of Mary, I offer You my prayers, works, joys and sufferings of this day for all the intentions of Your Sacred Heart, in union with the Holy Sacrifice of the Mass throughout the world, in reparation for my sins, for the intentions of all my relatives and friends, and in particular for the intentions of the Holy Father. Amen.

READ & WRITE IT: BIBLE VERSE

REFLECT: WHAT DOES THIS MEAN TO ME?

RESPOND: WHAT DO I SAY TO GOD ABOUT THIS?

REST IN MEDITATION: HOW IS GOD ASKING ME TO CHANGE?

Lectio Devina

1. Ask God to see your day and actions through His eyes
2. Thank Him
3. Review and meditate on your day and actions
4. Face your shortcomings
5. Ask God for guidance and pray about tomorrow

I'M THANKFUL FOR...   MY SINS & SHORTCOMINGS TODAY

Examen

Day 13   *Morning Prayer*

O Jesus, through the Immaculate Heart of Mary, I offer You my prayers, works, joys and sufferings of this day for all the intentions of Your Sacred Heart, in union with the Holy Sacrifice of the Mass throughout the world, in reparation for my sins, for the intentions of all my relatives and friends, and in particular for the intentions of the Holy Father. Amen.

READ & WRITE IT OUT: BIBLE VERSE

REFLECT: WHAT DOES THIS MEAN TO ME?

RESPOND: WHAT DO I SAY TO GOD ABOUT THIS?

REST IN MEDITATION: HOW IS GOD ASKING ME TO CHANGE?

1. Ask God to see your day and actions through His eyes
2. Thank Him
3. Review and meditate on your day and actions
4. Face your shortcomings
5. Ask God for guidance and pray about tomorrow

I'M THANKFUL FOR...

MY SINS & SHORTCOMINGS TODAY

Lectio Devina

Examen

Day 14   *Morning Prayer*

O Jesus, through the Immaculate Heart of Mary, I offer You my prayers, works, joys and sufferings of this day for all the intentions of Your Sacred Heart, in union with the Holy Sacrifice of the Mass throughout the world, in reparation for my sins, for the intentions of all my relatives and friends, and in particular for the intentions of the Holy Father. Amen.

READ & WRITE IT: BIBLE VERSE

REFLECT: WHAT DOES THIS MEAN TO ME?

RESPOND: WHAT DO I SAY TO GOD ABOUT THIS?

REST IN MEDITATION: HOW IS GOD ASKING ME TO CHANGE?

1. Ask God to see your day and actions through His eyes
2. Thank Him
3. Review and meditate on your day and actions
4. Face your shortcomings
5. Ask God for guidance and pray about tomorrow

I'M THANKFUL FOR...

MY SINS & SHORTCOMINGS TODAY

Lectio Devina

Examen

Day 15

O Jesus, through the Immaculate Heart of Mary, I offer You my prayers, works, joys and sufferings of this day for all the intentions of Your Sacred Heart, in union with the Holy Sacrifice of the Mass throughout the world, in reparation for my sins, for the intentions of all my relatives and friends, and in particular for the intentions of the Holy Father. Amen.

Lectio Devina

READ & WRITE IT OUT: BIBLE VERSE

REFLECT: WHAT DOES THIS MEAN TO ME?

RESPOND: WHAT DO I SAY TO GOD ABOUT THIS?

REST IN MEDITATION: HOW IS GOD ASKING ME TO CHANGE?

Examen

1. Ask God to see your day and actions through His eyes
2. Thank Him
3. Review and meditate on your day and actions
4. Face your shortcomings
5. Ask God for guidance and pray about tomorrow

I'M THANKFUL FOR...

MY SINS & SHORTCOMINGS TODAY

Day 16

Morning Prayer

O Jesus, through the Immaculate Heart of Mary, I offer You my prayers, works, joys and sufferings of this day for all the intentions of Your Sacred Heart, in union with the Holy Sacrifice of the Mass throughout the world, in reparation for my sins, for the intentions of all my relatives and friends, and in particular for the intentions of the Holy Father. Amen.

Lectio Devina

READ & WRITE IT: BIBLE VERSE

REFLECT: WHAT DOES THIS MEAN TO ME?

RESPOND: WHAT DO I SAY TO GOD ABOUT THIS?

REST IN MEDITATION: HOW IS GOD ASKING ME TO CHANGE?

Examen

1. Ask God to see your day and actions through His eyes
2. Thank Him
3. Review and meditate on your day and actions
4. Face your shortcomings
5. Ask God for guidance and pray about tomorrow

I'M THANKFUL FOR...

MY SINS & SHORTCOMINGS TODAY

Day 17

O Jesus, through the Immaculate Heart of Mary, I offer You my prayers, works, joys and sufferings of this day for all the intentions of Your Sacred Heart, in union with the Holy Sacrifice of the Mass throughout the world, in reparation for my sins, for the intentions of all my relatives and friends, and in particular for the intentions of the Holy Father. Amen.

Lectio Devina

READ & WRITE IT OUT: BIBLE VERSE

REFLECT: WHAT DOES THIS MEAN TO ME?

RESPOND: WHAT DO I SAY TO GOD ABOUT THIS?

REST IN MEDITATION: HOW IS GOD ASKING ME TO CHANGE?

Examen

1. Ask God to see your day and actions through His eyes
2. Thank Him
3. Review and meditate on your day and actions
4. Face your shortcomings
5. Ask God for guidance and pray about tomorrow

I'M THANKFUL FOR...

MY SINS & SHORTCOMINGS TODAY

Day 18

Morning Prayer

O Jesus, through the Immaculate Heart of Mary, I offer You my prayers, works, joys and sufferings of this day for all the intentions of Your Sacred Heart, in union with the Holy Sacrifice of the Mass throughout the world, in reparation for my sins, for the intentions of all my relatives and friends, and in particular for the intentions of the Holy Father. Amen.

Lectio Devina

READ & WRITE IT: BIBLE VERSE

REFLECT: WHAT DOES THIS MEAN TO ME?

RESPOND: WHAT DO I SAY TO GOD ABOUT THIS?

REST IN MEDITATION: HOW IS GOD ASKING ME TO CHANGE?

Examen

1. Ask God to see your day and actions through His eyes
2. Thank Him
3. Review and meditate on your day and actions
4. Face your shortcomings
5. Ask God for guidance and pray about tomorrow

I'M THANKFUL FOR...

MY SINS & SHORTCOMINGS TODAY

Day 19

O Jesus, through the Immaculate Heart of Mary, I offer You my prayers, works, joys and sufferings of this day for all the intentions of Your Sacred Heart, in union with the Holy Sacrifice of the Mass throughout the world, in reparation for my sins, for the intentions of all my relatives and friends, and in particular for the intentions of the Holy Father. Amen.

Lectio Devina

READ & WRITE IT OUT: BIBLE VERSE

REFLECT: WHAT DOES THIS MEAN TO ME?

RESPOND: WHAT DO I SAY TO GOD ABOUT THIS?

REST IN MEDITATION: HOW IS GOD ASKING ME TO CHANGE?

Examen

1. Ask God to see your day and actions through His eyes
2. Thank Him
3. Review and meditate on your day and actions
4. Face your shortcomings
5. Ask God for guidance and pray about tomorrow

I'M THANKFUL FOR...

MY SINS & SHORTCOMINGS TODAY

Day 20

Morning Prayer

O Jesus, through the Immaculate Heart of Mary, I offer You my prayers, works, joys and sufferings of this day for all the intentions of Your Sacred Heart, in union with the Holy Sacrifice of the Mass throughout the world, in reparation for my sins, for the intentions of all my relatives and friends, and in particular for the intentions of the Holy Father. Amen.

Lectio Devina

READ & WRITE IT: BIBLE VERSE

REFLECT: WHAT DOES THIS MEAN TO ME?

RESPOND: WHAT DO I SAY TO GOD ABOUT THIS?

REST IN MEDITATION: HOW IS GOD ASKING ME TO CHANGE?

Examen

1. Ask God to see your day and actions through His eyes
2. Thank Him
3. Review and meditate on your day and actions
4. Face your shortcomings
5. Ask God for guidance and pray about tomorrow

I'M THANKFUL FOR...

MY SINS & SHORTCOMINGS TODAY

Day 21   *Morning Prayer*

O Jesus, through the Immaculate Heart of Mary, I offer You my prayers, works, joys and sufferings of this day for all the intentions of Your Sacred Heart, in union with the Holy Sacrifice of the Mass throughout the world, in reparation for my sins, for the intentions of all my relatives and friends, and in particular for the intentions of the Holy Father. Amen.

READ & WRITE IT OUT: BIBLE VERSE

REFLECT: WHAT DOES THIS MEAN TO ME?

RESPOND: WHAT DO I SAY TO GOD ABOUT THIS?

REST IN MEDITATION: HOW IS GOD ASKING ME TO CHANGE?

1. Ask God to see your day and actions through His eyes
2. Thank Him
3. Review and meditate on your day and actions
4. Face your shortcomings
5. Ask God for guidance and pray about tomorrow

I'M THANKFUL FOR...   MY SINS & SHORTCOMINGS TODAY

Day 22   *Morning Prayer*

O Jesus, through the Immaculate Heart of Mary, I offer You my prayers, works, joys and sufferings of this day for all the intentions of Your Sacred Heart, in union with the Holy Sacrifice of the Mass throughout the world, in reparation for my sins, for the intentions of all my relatives and friends, and in particular for the intentions of the Holy Father. Amen.

READ & WRITE IT: BIBLE VERSE

REFLECT: WHAT DOES THIS MEAN TO ME?

RESPOND: WHAT DO I SAY TO GOD ABOUT THIS?

REST IN MEDITATION: HOW IS GOD ASKING ME TO CHANGE?

1. Ask God to see your day and actions through His eyes
2. Thank Him
3. Review and meditate on your day and actions
4. Face your shortcomings
5. Ask God for guidance and pray about tomorrow

I'M THANKFUL FOR...   MY SINS & SHORTCOMINGS TODAY

Day 23

O Jesus, through the Immaculate Heart of Mary, I offer You my prayers, works, joys and sufferings of this day for all the intentions of Your Sacred Heart, in union with the Holy Sacrifice of the Mass throughout the world, in reparation for my sins, for the intentions of all my relatives and friends, and in particular for the intentions of the Holy Father. Amen.

Lectio Devina

READ & WRITE IT OUT: BIBLE VERSE

REFLECT: WHAT DOES THIS MEAN TO ME?

RESPOND: WHAT DO I SAY TO GOD ABOUT THIS?

REST IN MEDITATION: HOW IS GOD ASKING ME TO CHANGE?

Examen

1. Ask God to see your day and actions through His eyes
2. Thank Him
3. Review and meditate on your day and actions
4. Face your shortcomings
5. Ask God for guidance and pray about tomorrow

I'M THANKFUL FOR...

MY SINS & SHORTCOMINGS TODAY

Day 24

Morning Prayer

O Jesus, through the Immaculate Heart of Mary, I offer You my prayers, works, joys and sufferings of this day for all the intentions of Your Sacred Heart, in union with the Holy Sacrifice of the Mass throughout the world, in reparation for my sins, for the intentions of all my relatives and friends, and in particular for the intentions of the Holy Father. Amen.

Lectio Devina

READ & WRITE IT: BIBLE VERSE

REFLECT: WHAT DOES THIS MEAN TO ME?

RESPOND: WHAT DO I SAY TO GOD ABOUT THIS?

REST IN MEDITATION: HOW IS GOD ASKING ME TO CHANGE?

Examen

1. Ask God to see your day and actions through His eyes
2. Thank Him
3. Review and meditate on your day and actions
4. Face your shortcomings
5. Ask God for guidance and pray about tomorrow

I'M THANKFUL FOR...

MY SINS & SHORTCOMINGS TODAY

Day 25

O Jesus, through the Immaculate Heart of Mary, I offer You my prayers, works, joys and sufferings of this day for all the intentions of Your Sacred Heart, in union with the Holy Sacrifice of the Mass throughout the world, in reparation for my sins, for the intentions of all my relatives and friends, and in particular for the intentions of the Holy Father. Amen.

Lectio Devina

READ & WRITE IT OUT: BIBLE VERSE

REFLECT: WHAT DOES THIS MEAN TO ME?

RESPOND: WHAT DO I SAY TO GOD ABOUT THIS?

REST IN MEDITATION: HOW IS GOD ASKING ME TO CHANGE?

Examen

1. Ask God to see your day and actions through His eyes
2. Thank Him
3. Review and meditate on your day and actions
4. Face your shortcomings
5. Ask God for guidance and pray about tomorrow

I'M THANKFUL FOR...

MY SINS & SHORTCOMINGS TODAY

Day 26

Morning Prayer

O Jesus, through the Immaculate Heart of Mary, I offer You my prayers, works, joys and sufferings of this day for all the intentions of Your Sacred Heart, in union with the Holy Sacrifice of the Mass throughout the world, in reparation for my sins, for the intentions of all my relatives and friends, and in particular for the intentions of the Holy Father. Amen.

Lectio Devina

READ & WRITE IT: BIBLE VERSE

REFLECT: WHAT DOES THIS MEAN TO ME?

RESPOND: WHAT DO I SAY TO GOD ABOUT THIS?

REST IN MEDITATION: HOW IS GOD ASKING ME TO CHANGE?

Examen

1. Ask God to see your day and actions through His eyes
2. Thank Him
3. Review and meditate on your day and actions
4. Face your shortcomings
5. Ask God for guidance and pray about tomorrow

I'M THANKFUL FOR...

MY SINS & SHORTCOMINGS TODAY

Day 27   *Morning Prayer*

O Jesus, through the Immaculate Heart of Mary, I offer You my prayers, works, joys and sufferings of this day for all the intentions of Your Sacred Heart, in union with the Holy Sacrifice of the Mass throughout the world, in reparation for my sins, for the intentions of all my relatives and friends, and in particular for the intentions of the Holy Father. Amen.

READ & WRITE IT OUT: BIBLE VERSE

Lectio Devina

REFLECT: WHAT DOES THIS MEAN TO ME?

RESPOND: WHAT DO I SAY TO GOD ABOUT THIS?

REST IN MEDITATION: HOW IS GOD ASKING ME TO CHANGE?

Examen

1. Ask God to see your day and actions through His eyes
2. Thank Him
3. Review and meditate on your day and actions
4. Face your shortcomings
5. Ask God for guidance and pray about tomorrow

I'M THANKFUL FOR...

MY SINS & SHORTCOMINGS TODAY

Day 28   *Morning Prayer*

O Jesus, through the Immaculate Heart of Mary, I offer You my prayers, works, joys and sufferings of this day for all the intentions of Your Sacred Heart, in union with the Holy Sacrifice of the Mass throughout the world, in reparation for my sins, for the intentions of all my relatives and friends, and in particular for the intentions of the Holy Father. Amen.

READ & WRITE IT: BIBLE VERSE

Lectio Devina

REFLECT: WHAT DOES THIS MEAN TO ME?

RESPOND: WHAT DO I SAY TO GOD ABOUT THIS?

REST IN MEDITATION: HOW IS GOD ASKING ME TO CHANGE?

Examen

1. Ask God to see your day and actions through His eyes
2. Thank Him
3. Review and meditate on your day and actions
4. Face your shortcomings
5. Ask God for guidance and pray about tomorrow

I'M THANKFUL FOR...

MY SINS & SHORTCOMINGS TODAY

Day 29

Morning Prayer

O Jesus, through the Immaculate Heart of Mary, I offer You my prayers, works, joys and sufferings of this day for all the intentions of Your Sacred Heart, in union with the Holy Sacrifice of the Mass throughout the world, in reparation for my sins, for the intentions of all my relatives and friends, and in particular for the intentions of the Holy Father. Amen.

READ & WRITE IT OUT: BIBLE VERSE

REFLECT: WHAT DOES THIS MEAN TO ME?

RESPOND: WHAT DO I SAY TO GOD ABOUT THIS?

REST IN MEDITATION: HOW IS GOD ASKING ME TO CHANGE?

Lectio Devina

1. Ask God to see your day and actions through His eyes
2. Thank Him
3. Review and meditate on your day and actions
4. Face your shortcomings
5. Ask God for guidance and pray about tomorrow

I'M THANKFUL FOR...

MY SINS & SHORTCOMINGS TODAY

Examen

Day 30

Morning Prayer

O Jesus, through the Immaculate Heart of Mary, I offer You my prayers, works, joys and sufferings of this day for all the intentions of Your Sacred Heart, in union with the Holy Sacrifice of the Mass throughout the world, in reparation for my sins, for the intentions of all my relatives and friends, and in particular for the intentions of the Holy Father. Amen.

READ & WRITE IT: BIBLE VERSE

REFLECT: WHAT DOES THIS MEAN TO ME?

RESPOND: WHAT DO I SAY TO GOD ABOUT THIS?

REST IN MEDITATION: HOW IS GOD ASKING ME TO CHANGE?

Lectio Devina

1. Ask God to see your day and actions through His eyes
2. Thank Him
3. Review and meditate on your day and actions
4. Face your shortcomings
5. Ask God for guidance and pray about tomorrow

I'M THANKFUL FOR...

MY SINS & SHORTCOMINGS TODAY

Examen

O Jesus, through the Immaculate Heart of Mary, I offer You my prayers, works, joys and sufferings of this day for all the intentions of Your Sacred Heart, in union with the Holy Sacrifice of the Mass throughout the world, in reparation for my sins, for the intentions of all my relatives and friends, and in particular for the intentions of the Holy Father. Amen.

Lectio Devina

READ & WRITE IT OUT: BIBLE VERSE

REFLECT: WHAT DOES THIS MEAN TO ME?

RESPOND: WHAT DO I SAY TO GOD ABOUT THIS?

REST IN MEDITATION: HOW IS GOD ASKING ME TO CHANGE?

Examen

1. Ask God to see your day and actions through His eyes
2. Thank Him
3. Review and meditate on your day and actions
4. Face your shortcomings
5. Ask God for guidance and pray about tomorrow

I'M THANKFUL FOR...

MY SINS & SHORTCOMINGS TODAY

PRAYERS & REFLECTIONS ON YOUR SPIRITUAL JOURNEY THIS MONTH

September

"Turn your eyes incessantly to the Blessed Virgin; she, who is the Mother of Sorrows and also the Mother of Consolation, can understand you completely and help you. Looking to her, praying to her, you will obtain that your tedium will become serenity, your anguish change into hope, and your grief into love. I accompany you with my blessing, which I willingly extend to all those who assist you." -Saint Pope John Paul the Great

PERSONAL RESOLUTIONS

SPIRITUAL READING LOG

LAST CONFESSION DATE

PRAYER REQUESTS

HOLY ACTIVITIES WITH MY FAMILY/ FRIENDS

ROSARY & CHAPLET TRACKER

"We are all called to be great saints; don't miss the opportunity!" - Mother Angelica

Day 1

Morning Prayer

O Jesus, through the Immaculate Heart of Mary, I offer You my prayers, works, joys and sufferings of this day for all the intentions of Your Sacred Heart, in union with the Holy Sacrifice of the Mass throughout the world, in reparation for my sins, for the intentions of all my relatives and friends, and in particular for the intentions of the Holy Father. Amen.

Lectio Devina

READ & WRITE IT OUT: BIBLE VERSE

REFLECT: WHAT DOES THIS MEAN TO ME?

RESPOND: WHAT DO I SAY TO GOD ABOUT THIS?

REST IN MEDITATION: HOW IS GOD ASKING ME TO CHANGE?

Examen

1. Ask God to see your day and actions through His eyes
2. Thank Him
3. Review and meditate on your day and actions
4. Face your shortcomings
5. Ask God for guidance and pray about tomorrow

I'M THANKFUL FOR...

MY SINS & SHORTCOMINGS TODAY

Day 2

Morning Prayer

O Jesus, through the Immaculate Heart of Mary, I offer You my prayers, works, joys and sufferings of this day for all the intentions of Your Sacred Heart, in union with the Holy Sacrifice of the Mass throughout the world, in reparation for my sins, for the intentions of all my relatives and friends, and in particular for the intentions of the Holy Father. Amen.

Lectio Devina

READ & WRITE IT: BIBLE VERSE

REFLECT: WHAT DOES THIS MEAN TO ME?

RESPOND: WHAT DO I SAY TO GOD ABOUT THIS?

REST IN MEDITATION: HOW IS GOD ASKING ME TO CHANGE?

Examen

1. Ask God to see your day and actions through His eyes
2. Thank Him
3. Review and meditate on your day and actions
4. Face your shortcomings
5. Ask God for guidance and pray about tomorrow

I'M THANKFUL FOR...

MY SINS & SHORTCOMINGS TODAY

Day 3

O Jesus, through the Immaculate Heart of Mary, I offer You my prayers, works, joys and sufferings of this day for all the intentions of Your Sacred Heart, in union with the Holy Sacrifice of the Mass throughout the world, in reparation for my sins, for the intentions of all my relatives and friends, and in particular for the intentions of the Holy Father. Amen.

Lectio Devina

READ & WRITE IT OUT: BIBLE VERSE

REFLECT: WHAT DOES THIS MEAN TO ME?

RESPOND: WHAT DO I SAY TO GOD ABOUT THIS?

REST IN MEDITATION: HOW IS GOD ASKING ME TO CHANGE?

Examen

1. Ask God to see your day and actions through His eyes
2. Thank Him
3. Review and meditate on your day and actions
4. Face your shortcomings
5. Ask God for guidance and pray about tomorrow

I'M THANKFUL FOR...

MY SINS & SHORTCOMINGS TODAY

Day 4

Morning Prayer

O Jesus, through the Immaculate Heart of Mary, I offer You my prayers, works, joys and sufferings of this day for all the intentions of Your Sacred Heart, in union with the Holy Sacrifice of the Mass throughout the world, in reparation for my sins, for the intentions of all my relatives and friends, and in particular for the intentions of the Holy Father. Amen.

Lectio Devina

READ & WRITE IT: BIBLE VERSE

REFLECT: WHAT DOES THIS MEAN TO ME?

RESPOND: WHAT DO I SAY TO GOD ABOUT THIS?

REST IN MEDITATION: HOW IS GOD ASKING ME TO CHANGE?

Examen

1. Ask God to see your day and actions through His eyes
2. Thank Him
3. Review and meditate on your day and actions
4. Face your shortcomings
5. Ask God for guidance and pray about tomorrow

I'M THANKFUL FOR...

MY SINS & SHORTCOMINGS TODAY

Day 5

O Jesus, through the Immaculate Heart of Mary, I offer You my prayers, works, joys and sufferings of this day for all the intentions of Your Sacred Heart, in union with the Holy Sacrifice of the Mass throughout the world, in reparation for my sins, for the intentions of all my relatives and friends, and in particular for the intentions of the Holy Father. Amen.

Lectio Devina

READ & WRITE IT OUT: BIBLE VERSE

REFLECT: WHAT DOES THIS MEAN TO ME?

RESPOND: WHAT DO I SAY TO GOD ABOUT THIS?

REST IN MEDITATION: HOW IS GOD ASKING ME TO CHANGE?

Examen

1. Ask God to see your day and actions through His eyes
2. Thank Him
3. Review and meditate on your day and actions
4. Face your shortcomings
5. Ask God for guidance and pray about tomorrow

I'M THANKFUL FOR...

MY SINS & SHORTCOMINGS TODAY

Day 6

Morning Prayer

O Jesus, through the Immaculate Heart of Mary, I offer You my prayers, works, joys and sufferings of this day for all the intentions of Your Sacred Heart, in union with the Holy Sacrifice of the Mass throughout the world, in reparation for my sins, for the intentions of all my relatives and friends, and in particular for the intentions of the Holy Father. Amen.

Lectio Devina

READ & WRITE IT: BIBLE VERSE

REFLECT: WHAT DOES THIS MEAN TO ME?

RESPOND: WHAT DO I SAY TO GOD ABOUT THIS?

REST IN MEDITATION: HOW IS GOD ASKING ME TO CHANGE?

Examen

1. Ask God to see your day and actions through His eyes
2. Thank Him
3. Review and meditate on your day and actions
4. Face your shortcomings
5. Ask God for guidance and pray about tomorrow

I'M THANKFUL FOR...

MY SINS & SHORTCOMINGS TODAY

Day 7   *Morning Prayer*

O Jesus, through the Immaculate Heart of Mary, I offer You my prayers, works, joys and sufferings of this day for all the intentions of Your Sacred Heart, in union with the Holy Sacrifice of the Mass throughout the world, in reparation for my sins, for the intentions of all my relatives and friends, and in particular for the intentions of the Holy Father. Amen.

READ & WRITE IT OUT: BIBLE VERSE

REFLECT: WHAT DOES THIS MEAN TO ME?

RESPOND: WHAT DO I SAY TO GOD ABOUT THIS?

REST IN MEDITATION: HOW IS GOD ASKING ME TO CHANGE?

Lectio Devina

1. Ask God to see your day and actions through His eyes
2. Thank Him
3. Review and meditate on your day and actions
4. Face your shortcomings
5. Ask God for guidance and pray about tomorrow

I'M THANKFUL FOR...

MY SINS & SHORTCOMINGS TODAY

Examen

Day 8   *Morning Prayer*

O Jesus, through the Immaculate Heart of Mary, I offer You my prayers, works, joys and sufferings of this day for all the intentions of Your Sacred Heart, in union with the Holy Sacrifice of the Mass throughout the world, in reparation for my sins, for the intentions of all my relatives and friends, and in particular for the intentions of the Holy Father. Amen.

READ & WRITE IT: BIBLE VERSE

REFLECT: WHAT DOES THIS MEAN TO ME?

RESPOND: WHAT DO I SAY TO GOD ABOUT THIS?

REST IN MEDITATION: HOW IS GOD ASKING ME TO CHANGE?

Lectio Devina

1. Ask God to see your day and actions through His eyes
2. Thank Him
3. Review and meditate on your day and actions
4. Face your shortcomings
5. Ask God for guidance and pray about tomorrow

I'M THANKFUL FOR...

MY SINS & SHORTCOMINGS TODAY

Examen

Day 9   *Morning Prayer*

O Jesus, through the Immaculate Heart of Mary, I offer You my prayers, works, joys and sufferings of this day for all the intentions of Your Sacred Heart, in union with the Holy Sacrifice of the Mass throughout the world, in reparation for my sins, for the intentions of all my relatives and friends, and in particular for the intentions of the Holy Father. Amen.

READ & WRITE IT OUT: BIBLE VERSE

REFLECT: WHAT DOES THIS MEAN TO ME?

RESPOND: WHAT DO I SAY TO GOD ABOUT THIS?

REST IN MEDITATION: HOW IS GOD ASKING ME TO CHANGE?

Lectio Devina

1. Ask God to see your day and actions through His eyes
2. Thank Him
3. Review and meditate on your day and actions
4. Face your shortcomings
5. Ask God for guidance and pray about tomorrow

I'M THANKFUL FOR...

MY SINS & SHORTCOMINGS TODAY

Examen

Day 10   *Morning Prayer*

O Jesus, through the Immaculate Heart of Mary, I offer You my prayers, works, joys and sufferings of this day for all the intentions of Your Sacred Heart, in union with the Holy Sacrifice of the Mass throughout the world, in reparation for my sins, for the intentions of all my relatives and friends, and in particular for the intentions of the Holy Father. Amen.

READ & WRITE IT: BIBLE VERSE

REFLECT: WHAT DOES THIS MEAN TO ME?

RESPOND: WHAT DO I SAY TO GOD ABOUT THIS?

REST IN MEDITATION: HOW IS GOD ASKING ME TO CHANGE?

Lectio Devina

1. Ask God to see your day and actions through His eyes
2. Thank Him
3. Review and meditate on your day and actions
4. Face your shortcomings
5. Ask God for guidance and pray about tomorrow

I'M THANKFUL FOR...

MY SINS & SHORTCOMINGS TODAY

Examen

Day 11

O Jesus, through the Immaculate Heart of Mary, I offer You my prayers, works, joys and sufferings of this day for all the intentions of Your Sacred Heart, in union with the Holy Sacrifice of the Mass throughout the world, in reparation for my sins, for the intentions of all my relatives and friends, and in particular for the intentions of the Holy Father. Amen.

READ & WRITE IT OUT: BIBLE VERSE

REFLECT: WHAT DOES THIS MEAN TO ME?

RESPOND: WHAT DO I SAY TO GOD ABOUT THIS?

REST IN MEDITATION: HOW IS GOD ASKING ME TO CHANGE?

Lectio Devina

1. Ask God to see your day and actions through His eyes
2. Thank Him
3. Review and meditate on your day and actions
4. Face your shortcomings
5. Ask God for guidance and pray about tomorrow

I'M THANKFUL FOR...

MY SINS & SHORTCOMINGS TODAY

Examen

Day 12

Morning Prayer

O Jesus, through the Immaculate Heart of Mary, I offer You my prayers, works, joys and sufferings of this day for all the intentions of Your Sacred Heart, in union with the Holy Sacrifice of the Mass throughout the world, in reparation for my sins, for the intentions of all my relatives and friends, and in particular for the intentions of the Holy Father. Amen.

READ & WRITE IT: BIBLE VERSE

REFLECT: WHAT DOES THIS MEAN TO ME?

RESPOND: WHAT DO I SAY TO GOD ABOUT THIS?

REST IN MEDITATION: HOW IS GOD ASKING ME TO CHANGE?

Lectio Devina

1. Ask God to see your day and actions through His eyes
2. Thank Him
3. Review and meditate on your day and actions
4. Face your shortcomings
5. Ask God for guidance and pray about tomorrow

I'M THANKFUL FOR...

MY SINS & SHORTCOMINGS TODAY

Examen

Day 13   *Morning Prayer*

O Jesus, through the Immaculate Heart of Mary, I offer You my prayers, works, joys and sufferings of this day for all the intentions of Your Sacred Heart, in union with the Holy Sacrifice of the Mass throughout the world, in reparation for my sins, for the intentions of all my relatives and friends, and in particular for the intentions of the Holy Father. Amen.

Lectio Devina

READ & WRITE IT OUT: BIBLE VERSE

REFLECT: WHAT DOES THIS MEAN TO ME?

RESPOND: WHAT DO I SAY TO GOD ABOUT THIS?

REST IN MEDITATION: HOW IS GOD ASKING ME TO CHANGE?

Examen

1. Ask God to see your day and actions through His eyes
2. Thank Him
3. Review and meditate on your day and actions
4. Face your shortcomings
5. Ask God for guidance and pray about tomorrow

I'M THANKFUL FOR...

MY SINS & SHORTCOMINGS TODAY

Day 14   *Morning Prayer*

O Jesus, through the Immaculate Heart of Mary, I offer You my prayers, works, joys and sufferings of this day for all the intentions of Your Sacred Heart, in union with the Holy Sacrifice of the Mass throughout the world, in reparation for my sins, for the intentions of all my relatives and friends, and in particular for the intentions of the Holy Father. Amen.

Lectio Devina

READ & WRITE IT: BIBLE VERSE

REFLECT: WHAT DOES THIS MEAN TO ME?

RESPOND: WHAT DO I SAY TO GOD ABOUT THIS?

REST IN MEDITATION: HOW IS GOD ASKING ME TO CHANGE?

Examen

1. Ask God to see your day and actions through His eyes
2. Thank Him
3. Review and meditate on your day and actions
4. Face your shortcomings
5. Ask God for guidance and pray about tomorrow

I'M THANKFUL FOR...

MY SINS & SHORTCOMINGS TODAY

Day 15   *Morning Prayer*

O Jesus, through the Immaculate Heart of Mary, I offer You my prayers, works, joys and sufferings of this day for all the intentions of Your Sacred Heart, in union with the Holy Sacrifice of the Mass throughout the world, in reparation for my sins, for the intentions of all my relatives and friends, and in particular for the intentions of the Holy Father. Amen.

READ & WRITE IT OUT: BIBLE VERSE

REFLECT: WHAT DOES THIS MEAN TO ME?

RESPOND: WHAT DO I SAY TO GOD ABOUT THIS?

REST IN MEDITATION: HOW IS GOD ASKING ME TO CHANGE?

Lectio Devina

1. Ask God to see your day and actions through His eyes
2. Thank Him
3. Review and meditate on your day and actions
4. Face your shortcomings
5. Ask God for guidance and pray about tomorrow

Examen

I'M THANKFUL FOR...

MY SINS & SHORTCOMINGS TODAY

Day 16   *Morning Prayer*

O Jesus, through the Immaculate Heart of Mary, I offer You my prayers, works, joys and sufferings of this day for all the intentions of Your Sacred Heart, in union with the Holy Sacrifice of the Mass throughout the world, in reparation for my sins, for the intentions of all my relatives and friends, and in particular for the intentions of the Holy Father. Amen.

READ & WRITE IT: BIBLE VERSE

REFLECT: WHAT DOES THIS MEAN TO ME?

RESPOND: WHAT DO I SAY TO GOD ABOUT THIS?

REST IN MEDITATION: HOW IS GOD ASKING ME TO CHANGE?

Lectio Devina

1. Ask God to see your day and actions through His eyes
2. Thank Him
3. Review and meditate on your day and actions
4. Face your shortcomings
5. Ask God for guidance and pray about tomorrow

Examen

I'M THANKFUL FOR...

MY SINS & SHORTCOMINGS TODAY

Day 17   *Morning Prayer*

O Jesus, through the Immaculate Heart of Mary, I offer You my prayers, works, joys and sufferings of this day for all the intentions of Your Sacred Heart, in union with the Holy Sacrifice of the Mass throughout the world, in reparation for my sins, for the intentions of all my relatives and friends, and in particular for the intentions of the Holy Father. Amen.

READ & WRITE IT OUT: BIBLE VERSE

REFLECT: WHAT DOES THIS MEAN TO ME?

RESPOND: WHAT DO I SAY TO GOD ABOUT THIS?

REST IN MEDITATION: HOW IS GOD ASKING ME TO CHANGE?

Lectio Devina

1. Ask God to see your day and actions through His eyes
2. Thank Him
3. Review and meditate on your day and actions
4. Face your shortcomings
5. Ask God for guidance and pray about tomorrow

Examen

I'M THANKFUL FOR...   MY SINS & SHORTCOMINGS TODAY

Day 18   *Morning Prayer*

O Jesus, through the Immaculate Heart of Mary, I offer You my prayers, works, joys and sufferings of this day for all the intentions of Your Sacred Heart, in union with the Holy Sacrifice of the Mass throughout the world, in reparation for my sins, for the intentions of all my relatives and friends, and in particular for the intentions of the Holy Father. Amen.

READ & WRITE IT: BIBLE VERSE

REFLECT: WHAT DOES THIS MEAN TO ME?

RESPOND: WHAT DO I SAY TO GOD ABOUT THIS?

REST IN MEDITATION: HOW IS GOD ASKING ME TO CHANGE?

Lectio Devina

1. Ask God to see your day and actions through His eyes
2. Thank Him
3. Review and meditate on your day and actions
4. Face your shortcomings
5. Ask God for guidance and pray about tomorrow

Examen

I'M THANKFUL FOR...   MY SINS & SHORTCOMINGS TODAY

Day 19   *Morning Prayer*

O Jesus, through the Immaculate Heart of Mary, I offer You my prayers, works, joys and sufferings of this day for all the intentions of Your Sacred Heart, in union with the Holy Sacrifice of the Mass throughout the world, in reparation for my sins, for the intentions of all my relatives and friends, and in particular for the intentions of the Holy Father. Amen.

READ & WRITE IT OUT: BIBLE VERSE

REFLECT: WHAT DOES THIS MEAN TO ME?

RESPOND: WHAT DO I SAY TO GOD ABOUT THIS?

REST IN MEDITATION: HOW IS GOD ASKING ME TO CHANGE?

Lectio Devina

1. Ask God to see your day and actions through His eyes
2. Thank Him
3. Review and meditate on your day and actions
4. Face your shortcomings
5. Ask God for guidance and pray about tomorrow

I'M THANKFUL FOR...

MY SINS & SHORTCOMINGS TODAY

Examen

Day 20   *Morning Prayer*

O Jesus, through the Immaculate Heart of Mary, I offer You my prayers, works, joys and sufferings of this day for all the intentions of Your Sacred Heart, in union with the Holy Sacrifice of the Mass throughout the world, in reparation for my sins, for the intentions of all my relatives and friends, and in particular for the intentions of the Holy Father. Amen.

READ & WRITE IT: BIBLE VERSE

REFLECT: WHAT DOES THIS MEAN TO ME?

RESPOND: WHAT DO I SAY TO GOD ABOUT THIS?

REST IN MEDITATION: HOW IS GOD ASKING ME TO CHANGE?

Lectio Devina

1. Ask God to see your day and actions through His eyes
2. Thank Him
3. Review and meditate on your day and actions
4. Face your shortcomings
5. Ask God for guidance and pray about tomorrow

I'M THANKFUL FOR...

MY SINS & SHORTCOMINGS TODAY

Examen

Day 21

O Jesus, through the Immaculate Heart of Mary, I offer You my prayers, works, joys and sufferings of this day for all the intentions of Your Sacred Heart, in union with the Holy Sacrifice of the Mass throughout the world, in reparation for my sins, for the intentions of all my relatives and friends, and in particular for the intentions of the Holy Father. Amen.

Lectio Devina

READ & WRITE IT OUT: BIBLE VERSE

REFLECT: WHAT DOES THIS MEAN TO ME?

RESPOND: WHAT DO I SAY TO GOD ABOUT THIS?

REST IN MEDITATION: HOW IS GOD ASKING ME TO CHANGE?

Examen

1. Ask God to see your day and actions through His eyes
2. Thank Him
3. Review and meditate on your day and actions
4. Face your shortcomings
5. Ask God for guidance and pray about tomorrow

I'M THANKFUL FOR...

MY SINS & SHORTCOMINGS TODAY

Day 22

Morning Prayer

O Jesus, through the Immaculate Heart of Mary, I offer You my prayers, works, joys and sufferings of this day for all the intentions of Your Sacred Heart, in union with the Holy Sacrifice of the Mass throughout the world, in reparation for my sins, for the intentions of all my relatives and friends, and in particular for the intentions of the Holy Father. Amen.

Lectio Devina

READ & WRITE IT: BIBLE VERSE

REFLECT: WHAT DOES THIS MEAN TO ME?

RESPOND: WHAT DO I SAY TO GOD ABOUT THIS?

REST IN MEDITATION: HOW IS GOD ASKING ME TO CHANGE?

Examen

1. Ask God to see your day and actions through His eyes
2. Thank Him
3. Review and meditate on your day and actions
4. Face your shortcomings
5. Ask God for guidance and pray about tomorrow

I'M THANKFUL FOR...

MY SINS & SHORTCOMINGS TODAY

Day 23

Morning Prayer

O Jesus, through the Immaculate Heart of Mary, I offer You my prayers, works, joys and sufferings of this day for all the intentions of Your Sacred Heart, in union with the Holy Sacrifice of the Mass throughout the world, in reparation for my sins, for the intentions of all my relatives and friends, and in particular for the intentions of the Holy Father. Amen.

Lectio Devina

READ & WRITE IT OUT: BIBLE VERSE

REFLECT: WHAT DOES THIS MEAN TO ME?

RESPOND: WHAT DO I SAY TO GOD ABOUT THIS?

REST IN MEDITATION: HOW IS GOD ASKING ME TO CHANGE?

Examen

1. Ask God to see your day and actions through His eyes
2. Thank Him
3. Review and meditate on your day and actions
4. Face your shortcomings
5. Ask God for guidance and pray about tomorrow

I'M THANKFUL FOR...

MY SINS & SHORTCOMINGS TODAY

Day 24

Morning Prayer

O Jesus, through the Immaculate Heart of Mary, I offer You my prayers, works, joys and sufferings of this day for all the intentions of Your Sacred Heart, in union with the Holy Sacrifice of the Mass throughout the world, in reparation for my sins, for the intentions of all my relatives and friends, and in particular for the intentions of the Holy Father. Amen.

Lectio Devina

READ & WRITE IT: BIBLE VERSE

REFLECT: WHAT DOES THIS MEAN TO ME?

RESPOND: WHAT DO I SAY TO GOD ABOUT THIS?

REST IN MEDITATION: HOW IS GOD ASKING ME TO CHANGE?

Examen

1. Ask God to see your day and actions through His eyes
2. Thank Him
3. Review and meditate on your day and actions
4. Face your shortcomings
5. Ask God for guidance and pray about tomorrow

I'M THANKFUL FOR...

MY SINS & SHORTCOMINGS TODAY

Day 25   *Morning Prayer*

O Jesus, through the Immaculate Heart of Mary, I offer You my prayers, works, joys and sufferings of this day for all the intentions of Your Sacred Heart, in union with the Holy Sacrifice of the Mass throughout the world, in reparation for my sins, for the intentions of all my relatives and friends, and in particular for the intentions of the Holy Father. Amen.

READ & WRITE IT OUT: BIBLE VERSE

REFLECT: WHAT DOES THIS MEAN TO ME?

RESPOND: WHAT DO I SAY TO GOD ABOUT THIS?

REST IN MEDITATION: HOW IS GOD ASKING ME TO CHANGE?

Lectio Devina

1. Ask God to see your day and actions through His eyes
2. Thank Him
3. Review and meditate on your day and actions
4. Face your shortcomings
5. Ask God for guidance and pray about tomorrow

I'M THANKFUL FOR...

MY SINS & SHORTCOMINGS TODAY

Examen

Day 26   *Morning Prayer*

O Jesus, through the Immaculate Heart of Mary, I offer You my prayers, works, joys and sufferings of this day for all the intentions of Your Sacred Heart, in union with the Holy Sacrifice of the Mass throughout the world, in reparation for my sins, for the intentions of all my relatives and friends, and in particular for the intentions of the Holy Father. Amen.

READ & WRITE IT: BIBLE VERSE

REFLECT: WHAT DOES THIS MEAN TO ME?

RESPOND: WHAT DO I SAY TO GOD ABOUT THIS?

REST IN MEDITATION: HOW IS GOD ASKING ME TO CHANGE?

Lectio Devina

1. Ask God to see your day and actions through His eyes
2. Thank Him
3. Review and meditate on your day and actions
4. Face your shortcomings
5. Ask God for guidance and pray about tomorrow

I'M THANKFUL FOR...

MY SINS & SHORTCOMINGS TODAY

Examen

Day 27   *Morning Prayer*

O Jesus, through the Immaculate Heart of Mary, I offer You my prayers, works, joys and sufferings of this day for all the intentions of Your Sacred Heart, in union with the Holy Sacrifice of the Mass throughout the world, in reparation for my sins, for the intentions of all my relatives and friends, and in particular for the intentions of the Holy Father. Amen.

READ & WRITE IT OUT: BIBLE VERSE

Lectio Devina

REFLECT: WHAT DOES THIS MEAN TO ME?

RESPOND: WHAT DO I SAY TO GOD ABOUT THIS?

REST IN MEDITATION: HOW IS GOD ASKING ME TO CHANGE?

Examen

1. Ask God to see your day and actions through His eyes	I'M THANKFUL FOR...	MY SINS & SHORTCOMINGS TODAY
2. Thank Him		
3. Review and meditate on your day and actions		
4. Face your shortcomings		
5. Ask God for guidance and pray about tomorrow		

Day 28   *Morning Prayer*

O Jesus, through the Immaculate Heart of Mary, I offer You my prayers, works, joys and sufferings of this day for all the intentions of Your Sacred Heart, in union with the Holy Sacrifice of the Mass throughout the world, in reparation for my sins, for the intentions of all my relatives and friends, and in particular for the intentions of the Holy Father. Amen.

READ & WRITE IT: BIBLE VERSE

Lectio Devina

REFLECT: WHAT DOES THIS MEAN TO ME?

RESPOND: WHAT DO I SAY TO GOD ABOUT THIS?

REST IN MEDITATION: HOW IS GOD ASKING ME TO CHANGE?

Examen

1. Ask God to see your day and actions through His eyes	I'M THANKFUL FOR...	MY SINS & SHORTCOMINGS TODAY
2. Thank Him		
3. Review and meditate on your day and actions		
4. Face your shortcomings		
5. Ask God for guidance and pray about tomorrow		

Day 29   *Morning Prayer*

O Jesus, through the Immaculate Heart of Mary, I offer You my prayers, works, joys and sufferings of this day for all the intentions of Your Sacred Heart, in union with the Holy Sacrifice of the Mass throughout the world, in reparation for my sins, for the intentions of all my relatives and friends, and in particular for the intentions of the Holy Father. Amen.

READ & WRITE IT OUT: BIBLE VERSE

REFLECT: WHAT DOES THIS MEAN TO ME?

RESPOND: WHAT DO I SAY TO GOD ABOUT THIS?

REST IN MEDITATION: HOW IS GOD ASKING ME TO CHANGE?

Lectio Devina

1. Ask God to see your day and actions through His eyes
2. Thank Him
3. Review and meditate on your day and actions
4. Face your shortcomings
5. Ask God for guidance and pray about tomorrow

I'M THANKFUL FOR...   MY SINS & SHORTCOMINGS TODAY

Examen

Day 30   *Morning Prayer*

O Jesus, through the Immaculate Heart of Mary, I offer You my prayers, works, joys and sufferings of this day for all the intentions of Your Sacred Heart, in union with the Holy Sacrifice of the Mass throughout the world, in reparation for my sins, for the intentions of all my relatives and friends, and in particular for the intentions of the Holy Father. Amen.

READ & WRITE IT: BIBLE VERSE

REFLECT: WHAT DOES THIS MEAN TO ME?

RESPOND: WHAT DO I SAY TO GOD ABOUT THIS?

REST IN MEDITATION: HOW IS GOD ASKING ME TO CHANGE?

Lectio Devina

1. Ask God to see your day and actions through His eyes
2. Thank Him
3. Review and meditate on your day and actions
4. Face your shortcomings
5. Ask God for guidance and pray about tomorrow

I'M THANKFUL FOR...   MY SINS & SHORTCOMINGS TODAY

Examen

PRAYERS & REFLECTIONS ON YOUR SPIRITUAL JOURNEY THIS MONTH

Jesus, I trust in You!

October

"Say the Holy Rosary. Blessed be that monotony of Hail Marys which purifies the monotony of your sins!" -St. Josemaria Escriva

PERSONAL RESOLUTIONS

SPIRITUAL READING LOG

LAST CONFESSION DATE

HOLY ACTIVITIES WITH MY FAMILY/ FRIENDS

PRAYER REQUESTS

ROSARY & CHAPLET TRACKER

"We are all called to be great saints; don't miss the opportunity!" - Mother Angelica

Day 1

Morning Prayer

O Jesus, through the Immaculate Heart of Mary, I offer You my prayers, works, joys and sufferings of this day for all the intentions of Your Sacred Heart, in union with the Holy Sacrifice of the Mass throughout the world, in reparation for my sins, for the intentions of all my relatives and friends, and in particular for the intentions of the Holy Father. Amen.

READ & WRITE IT OUT: BIBLE VERSE

REFLECT: WHAT DOES THIS MEAN TO ME?

RESPOND: WHAT DO I SAY TO GOD ABOUT THIS?

REST IN MEDITATION: HOW IS GOD ASKING ME TO CHANGE?

Lectio Devina

1. Ask God to see your day and actions through His eyes 2. Thank Him 3. Review and meditate on your day and actions 4. Face your shortcomings 5. Ask God for guidance and pray about tomorrow	I'M THANKFUL FOR...	MY SINS & SHORTCOMINGS TODAY

Examen

Day 2

Morning Prayer

O Jesus, through the Immaculate Heart of Mary, I offer You my prayers, works, joys and sufferings of this day for all the intentions of Your Sacred Heart, in union with the Holy Sacrifice of the Mass throughout the world, in reparation for my sins, for the intentions of all my relatives and friends, and in particular for the intentions of the Holy Father. Amen.

READ & WRITE IT: BIBLE VERSE

REFLECT: WHAT DOES THIS MEAN TO ME?

RESPOND: WHAT DO I SAY TO GOD ABOUT THIS?

REST IN MEDITATION: HOW IS GOD ASKING ME TO CHANGE?

Lectio Devina

1. Ask God to see your day and actions through His eyes 2. Thank Him 3. Review and meditate on your day and actions 4. Face your shortcomings 5. Ask God for guidance and pray about tomorrow	I'M THANKFUL FOR...	MY SINS & SHORTCOMINGS TODAY

Examen

Day 3

O Jesus, through the Immaculate Heart of Mary, I offer You my prayers, works, joys and sufferings of this day for all the intentions of Your Sacred Heart, in union with the Holy Sacrifice of the Mass throughout the world, in reparation for my sins, for the intentions of all my relatives and friends, and in particular for the intentions of the Holy Father. Amen.

Lectio Devina

READ & WRITE IT OUT: BIBLE VERSE

REFLECT: WHAT DOES THIS MEAN TO ME?

RESPOND: WHAT DO I SAY TO GOD ABOUT THIS?

REST IN MEDITATION: HOW IS GOD ASKING ME TO CHANGE?

Examen

1. Ask God to see your day and actions through His eyes
2. Thank Him
3. Review and meditate on your day and actions
4. Face your shortcomings
5. Ask God for guidance and pray about tomorrow

I'M THANKFUL FOR...

MY SINS & SHORTCOMINGS TODAY

Day 4

Morning Prayer

O Jesus, through the Immaculate Heart of Mary, I offer You my prayers, works, joys and sufferings of this day for all the intentions of Your Sacred Heart, in union with the Holy Sacrifice of the Mass throughout the world, in reparation for my sins, for the intentions of all my relatives and friends, and in particular for the intentions of the Holy Father. Amen.

Lectio Devina

READ & WRITE IT: BIBLE VERSE

REFLECT: WHAT DOES THIS MEAN TO ME?

RESPOND: WHAT DO I SAY TO GOD ABOUT THIS?

REST IN MEDITATION: HOW IS GOD ASKING ME TO CHANGE?

Examen

1. Ask God to see your day and actions through His eyes
2. Thank Him
3. Review and meditate on your day and actions
4. Face your shortcomings
5. Ask God for guidance and pray about tomorrow

I'M THANKFUL FOR...

MY SINS & SHORTCOMINGS TODAY

Day 5

Morning Prayer

O Jesus, through the Immaculate Heart of Mary, I offer You my prayers, works, joys and sufferings of this day for all the intentions of Your Sacred Heart, in union with the Holy Sacrifice of the Mass throughout the world, in reparation for my sins, for the intentions of all my relatives and friends, and in particular for the intentions of the Holy Father. Amen.

READ & WRITE IT OUT: BIBLE VERSE

REFLECT: WHAT DOES THIS MEAN TO ME?

RESPOND: WHAT DO I SAY TO GOD ABOUT THIS?

REST IN MEDITATION: HOW IS GOD ASKING ME TO CHANGE?

Lectio Devina

1. Ask God to see your day and actions through His eyes
2. Thank Him
3. Review and meditate on your day and actions
4. Face your shortcomings
5. Ask God for guidance and pray about tomorrow

I'M THANKFUL FOR...

MY SINS & SHORTCOMINGS TODAY

Examen

Day 6

Morning Prayer

O Jesus, through the Immaculate Heart of Mary, I offer You my prayers, works, joys and sufferings of this day for all the intentions of Your Sacred Heart, in union with the Holy Sacrifice of the Mass throughout the world, in reparation for my sins, for the intentions of all my relatives and friends, and in particular for the intentions of the Holy Father. Amen.

READ & WRITE IT: BIBLE VERSE

REFLECT: WHAT DOES THIS MEAN TO ME?

RESPOND: WHAT DO I SAY TO GOD ABOUT THIS?

REST IN MEDITATION: HOW IS GOD ASKING ME TO CHANGE?

Lectio Devina

1. Ask God to see your day and actions through His eyes
2. Thank Him
3. Review and meditate on your day and actions
4. Face your shortcomings
5. Ask God for guidance and pray about tomorrow

I'M THANKFUL FOR...

MY SINS & SHORTCOMINGS TODAY

Examen

Day 7   *Morning Prayer*

O Jesus, through the Immaculate Heart of Mary, I offer You my prayers, works, joys and sufferings of this day for all the intentions of Your Sacred Heart, in union with the Holy Sacrifice of the Mass throughout the world, in reparation for my sins, for the intentions of all my relatives and friends, and in particular for the intentions of the Holy Father. Amen.

READ & WRITE IT OUT: BIBLE VERSE

REFLECT: WHAT DOES THIS MEAN TO ME?

RESPOND: WHAT DO I SAY TO GOD ABOUT THIS?

REST IN MEDITATION: HOW IS GOD ASKING ME TO CHANGE?

Lectio Devina

1. Ask God to see your day and actions through His eyes
2. Thank Him
3. Review and meditate on your day and actions
4. Face your shortcomings
5. Ask God for guidance and pray about tomorrow

I'M THANKFUL FOR...

MY SINS & SHORTCOMINGS TODAY

Examen

Day 8   *Morning Prayer*

O Jesus, through the Immaculate Heart of Mary, I offer You my prayers, works, joys and sufferings of this day for all the intentions of Your Sacred Heart, in union with the Holy Sacrifice of the Mass throughout the world, in reparation for my sins, for the intentions of all my relatives and friends, and in particular for the intentions of the Holy Father. Amen.

READ & WRITE IT: BIBLE VERSE

REFLECT: WHAT DOES THIS MEAN TO ME?

RESPOND: WHAT DO I SAY TO GOD ABOUT THIS?

REST IN MEDITATION: HOW IS GOD ASKING ME TO CHANGE?

Lectio Devina

1. Ask God to see your day and actions through His eyes
2. Thank Him
3. Review and meditate on your day and actions
4. Face your shortcomings
5. Ask God for guidance and pray about tomorrow

I'M THANKFUL FOR...

MY SINS & SHORTCOMINGS TODAY

Examen

Day 9   *Morning Prayer*

O Jesus, through the Immaculate Heart of Mary, I offer You my prayers, works, joys and sufferings of this day for all the intentions of Your Sacred Heart, in union with the Holy Sacrifice of the Mass throughout the world, in reparation for my sins, for the intentions of all my relatives and friends, and in particular for the intentions of the Holy Father. Amen.

READ & WRITE IT OUT: BIBLE VERSE

REFLECT: WHAT DOES THIS MEAN TO ME?

RESPOND: WHAT DO I SAY TO GOD ABOUT THIS?

REST IN MEDITATION: HOW IS GOD ASKING ME TO CHANGE?

	I'M THANKFUL FOR...	MY SINS & SHORTCOMINGS TODAY

1. Ask God to see your day and actions through His eyes
2. Thank Him
3. Review and meditate on your day and actions
4. Face your shortcomings
5. Ask God for guidance and pray about tomorrow

Day 10   *Morning Prayer*

O Jesus, through the Immaculate Heart of Mary, I offer You my prayers, works, joys and sufferings of this day for all the intentions of Your Sacred Heart, in union with the Holy Sacrifice of the Mass throughout the world, in reparation for my sins, for the intentions of all my relatives and friends, and in particular for the intentions of the Holy Father. Amen.

READ & WRITE IT: BIBLE VERSE

REFLECT: WHAT DOES THIS MEAN TO ME?

RESPOND: WHAT DO I SAY TO GOD ABOUT THIS?

REST IN MEDITATION: HOW IS GOD ASKING ME TO CHANGE?

	I'M THANKFUL FOR...	MY SINS & SHORTCOMINGS TODAY

1. Ask God to see your day and actions through His eyes
2. Thank Him
3. Review and meditate on your day and actions
4. Face your shortcomings
5. Ask God for guidance and pray about tomorrow

Day 11

O Jesus, through the Immaculate Heart of Mary, I offer You my prayers, works, joys and sufferings of this day for all the intentions of Your Sacred Heart, in union with the Holy Sacrifice of the Mass throughout the world, in reparation for my sins, for the intentions of all my relatives and friends, and in particular for the intentions of the Holy Father. Amen.

Lectio Devina

READ & WRITE IT OUT: BIBLE VERSE

REFLECT: WHAT DOES THIS MEAN TO ME?

RESPOND: WHAT DO I SAY TO GOD ABOUT THIS?

REST IN MEDITATION: HOW IS GOD ASKING ME TO CHANGE?

Examen

1. Ask God to see your day and actions through His eyes
2. Thank Him
3. Review and meditate on your day and actions
4. Face your shortcomings
5. Ask God for guidance and pray about tomorrow

I'M THANKFUL FOR...

MY SINS & SHORTCOMINGS TODAY

Day 12

Morning Prayer

O Jesus, through the Immaculate Heart of Mary, I offer You my prayers, works, joys and sufferings of this day for all the intentions of Your Sacred Heart, in union with the Holy Sacrifice of the Mass throughout the world, in reparation for my sins, for the intentions of all my relatives and friends, and in particular for the intentions of the Holy Father. Amen.

Lectio Devina

READ & WRITE IT: BIBLE VERSE

REFLECT: WHAT DOES THIS MEAN TO ME?

RESPOND: WHAT DO I SAY TO GOD ABOUT THIS?

REST IN MEDITATION: HOW IS GOD ASKING ME TO CHANGE?

Examen

1. Ask God to see your day and actions through His eyes
2. Thank Him
3. Review and meditate on your day and actions
4. Face your shortcomings
5. Ask God for guidance and pray about tomorrow

I'M THANKFUL FOR...

MY SINS & SHORTCOMINGS TODAY

Day 13

Morning Prayer

Morning Prayer

O Jesus, through the Immaculate Heart of Mary, I offer You my prayers, works, joys and sufferings of this day for all the intentions of Your Sacred Heart, in union with the Holy Sacrifice of the Mass throughout the world, in reparation for my sins, for the intentions of all my relatives and friends, and in particular for the intentions of the Holy Father. Amen.

READ & WRITE IT OUT: BIBLE VERSE

REFLECT: WHAT DOES THIS MEAN TO ME?

RESPOND: WHAT DO I SAY TO GOD ABOUT THIS?

REST IN MEDITATION: HOW IS GOD ASKING ME TO CHANGE?

Lectio Devina

1. Ask God to see your day and actions through His eyes
2. Thank Him
3. Review and meditate on your day and actions
4. Face your shortcomings
5. Ask God for guidance and pray about tomorrow

Examen

I'M THANKFUL FOR...

MY SINS & SHORTCOMINGS TODAY

Day 14

Morning Prayer

O Jesus, through the Immaculate Heart of Mary, I offer You my prayers, works, joys and sufferings of this day for all the intentions of Your Sacred Heart, in union with the Holy Sacrifice of the Mass throughout the world, in reparation for my sins, for the intentions of all my relatives and friends, and in particular for the intentions of the Holy Father. Amen.

READ & WRITE IT: BIBLE VERSE

REFLECT: WHAT DOES THIS MEAN TO ME?

RESPOND: WHAT DO I SAY TO GOD ABOUT THIS?

REST IN MEDITATION: HOW IS GOD ASKING ME TO CHANGE?

Lectio Devina

1. Ask God to see your day and actions through His eyes
2. Thank Him
3. Review and meditate on your day and actions
4. Face your shortcomings
5. Ask God for guidance and pray about tomorrow

Examen

I'M THANKFUL FOR...

MY SINS & SHORTCOMINGS TODAY

Day 15   *Morning Prayer*

O Jesus, through the Immaculate Heart of Mary, I offer You my prayers, works, joys and sufferings of this day for all the intentions of Your Sacred Heart, in union with the Holy Sacrifice of the Mass throughout the world, in reparation for my sins, for the intentions of all my relatives and friends, and in particular for the intentions of the Holy Father. Amen.

Lectio Devina

READ & WRITE IT OUT: BIBLE VERSE

REFLECT: WHAT DOES THIS MEAN TO ME?

RESPOND: WHAT DO I SAY TO GOD ABOUT THIS?

REST IN MEDITATION: HOW IS GOD ASKING ME TO CHANGE?

Examen

1. Ask God to see your day and actions through His eyes
2. Thank Him
3. Review and meditate on your day and actions
4. Face your shortcomings
5. Ask God for guidance and pray about tomorrow

I'M THANKFUL FOR...

MY SINS & SHORTCOMINGS TODAY

Day 16   *Morning Prayer*

O Jesus, through the Immaculate Heart of Mary, I offer You my prayers, works, joys and sufferings of this day for all the intentions of Your Sacred Heart, in union with the Holy Sacrifice of the Mass throughout the world, in reparation for my sins, for the intentions of all my relatives and friends, and in particular for the intentions of the Holy Father. Amen.

Lectio Devina

READ & WRITE IT: BIBLE VERSE

REFLECT: WHAT DOES THIS MEAN TO ME?

RESPOND: WHAT DO I SAY TO GOD ABOUT THIS?

REST IN MEDITATION: HOW IS GOD ASKING ME TO CHANGE?

Examen

1. Ask God to see your day and actions through His eyes
2. Thank Him
3. Review and meditate on your day and actions
4. Face your shortcomings
5. Ask God for guidance and pray about tomorrow

I'M THANKFUL FOR...

MY SINS & SHORTCOMINGS TODAY

Day 17

O Jesus, through the Immaculate Heart of Mary, I offer You my prayers, works, joys and sufferings of this day for all the intentions of Your Sacred Heart, in union with the Holy Sacrifice of the Mass throughout the world, in reparation for my sins, for the intentions of all my relatives and friends, and in particular for the intentions of the Holy Father. Amen.

READ & WRITE IT OUT: BIBLE VERSE

REFLECT: WHAT DOES THIS MEAN TO ME?

RESPOND: WHAT DO I SAY TO GOD ABOUT THIS?

REST IN MEDITATION: HOW IS GOD ASKING ME TO CHANGE?

Lectio Devina

1. Ask God to see your day and actions through His eyes
2. Thank Him
3. Review and meditate on your day and actions
4. Face your shortcomings
5. Ask God for guidance and pray about tomorrow

Examen

I'M THANKFUL FOR...

MY SINS & SHORTCOMINGS TODAY

Day 18

Morning Prayer

O Jesus, through the Immaculate Heart of Mary, I offer You my prayers, works, joys and sufferings of this day for all the intentions of Your Sacred Heart, in union with the Holy Sacrifice of the Mass throughout the world, in reparation for my sins, for the intentions of all my relatives and friends, and in particular for the intentions of the Holy Father. Amen.

READ & WRITE IT: BIBLE VERSE

REFLECT: WHAT DOES THIS MEAN TO ME?

RESPOND: WHAT DO I SAY TO GOD ABOUT THIS?

REST IN MEDITATION: HOW IS GOD ASKING ME TO CHANGE?

Lectio Devina

1. Ask God to see your day and actions through His eyes
2. Thank Him
3. Review and meditate on your day and actions
4. Face your shortcomings
5. Ask God for guidance and pray about tomorrow

Examen

I'M THANKFUL FOR...

MY SINS & SHORTCOMINGS TODAY

Day 19

Morning Prayer

O Jesus, through the Immaculate Heart of Mary, I offer You my prayers, works, joys and sufferings of this day for all the intentions of Your Sacred Heart, in union with the Holy Sacrifice of the Mass throughout the world, in reparation for my sins, for the intentions of all my relatives and friends, and in particular for the intentions of the Holy Father. Amen.

Lectio Devina

READ & WRITE IT OUT: BIBLE VERSE

REFLECT: WHAT DOES THIS MEAN TO ME?

RESPOND: WHAT DO I SAY TO GOD ABOUT THIS?

REST IN MEDITATION: HOW IS GOD ASKING ME TO CHANGE?

Examen

1. Ask God to see your day and actions through His eyes
2. Thank Him
3. Review and meditate on your day and actions
4. Face your shortcomings
5. Ask God for guidance and pray about tomorrow

I'M THANKFUL FOR...

MY SINS & SHORTCOMINGS TODAY

Day 20

Morning Prayer

O Jesus, through the Immaculate Heart of Mary, I offer You my prayers, works, joys and sufferings of this day for all the intentions of Your Sacred Heart, in union with the Holy Sacrifice of the Mass throughout the world, in reparation for my sins, for the intentions of all my relatives and friends, and in particular for the intentions of the Holy Father. Amen.

Lectio Devina

READ & WRITE IT: BIBLE VERSE

REFLECT: WHAT DOES THIS MEAN TO ME?

RESPOND: WHAT DO I SAY TO GOD ABOUT THIS?

REST IN MEDITATION: HOW IS GOD ASKING ME TO CHANGE?

Examen

1. Ask God to see your day and actions through His eyes
2. Thank Him
3. Review and meditate on your day and actions
4. Face your shortcomings
5. Ask God for guidance and pray about tomorrow

I'M THANKFUL FOR...

MY SINS & SHORTCOMINGS TODAY

Day 21

Morning Prayer

O Jesus, through the Immaculate Heart of Mary, I offer You my prayers, works, joys and sufferings of this day for all the intentions of Your Sacred Heart, in union with the Holy Sacrifice of the Mass throughout the world, in reparation for my sins, for the intentions of all my relatives and friends, and in particular for the intentions of the Holy Father. Amen.

READ & WRITE IT OUT: BIBLE VERSE

REFLECT: WHAT DOES THIS MEAN TO ME?

RESPOND: WHAT DO I SAY TO GOD ABOUT THIS?

REST IN MEDITATION: HOW IS GOD ASKING ME TO CHANGE?

Lectio Devina

1. Ask God to see your day and actions through His eyes
2. Thank Him
3. Review and meditate on your day and actions
4. Face your shortcomings
5. Ask God for guidance and pray about tomorrow

Examen

I'M THANKFUL FOR...

MY SINS & SHORTCOMINGS TODAY

Day 22

Morning Prayer

O Jesus, through the Immaculate Heart of Mary, I offer You my prayers, works, joys and sufferings of this day for all the intentions of Your Sacred Heart, in union with the Holy Sacrifice of the Mass throughout the world, in reparation for my sins, for the intentions of all my relatives and friends, and in particular for the intentions of the Holy Father. Amen.

READ & WRITE IT: BIBLE VERSE

REFLECT: WHAT DOES THIS MEAN TO ME?

RESPOND: WHAT DO I SAY TO GOD ABOUT THIS?

REST IN MEDITATION: HOW IS GOD ASKING ME TO CHANGE?

Lectio Devina

1. Ask God to see your day and actions through His eyes
2. Thank Him
3. Review and meditate on your day and actions
4. Face your shortcomings
5. Ask God for guidance and pray about tomorrow

Examen

I'M THANKFUL FOR...

MY SINS & SHORTCOMINGS TODAY

Day 23   *Morning Prayer*

O Jesus, through the Immaculate Heart of Mary, I offer You my prayers, works, joys and sufferings of this day for all the intentions of Your Sacred Heart, in union with the Holy Sacrifice of the Mass throughout the world, in reparation for my sins, for the intentions of all my relatives and friends, and in particular for the intentions of the Holy Father. Amen.

READ & WRITE IT OUT: BIBLE VERSE

REFLECT: WHAT DOES THIS MEAN TO ME?

RESPOND: WHAT DO I SAY TO GOD ABOUT THIS?

REST IN MEDITATION: HOW IS GOD ASKING ME TO CHANGE?

Lectio Devina

1. Ask God to see your day and actions through His eyes
2. Thank Him
3. Review and meditate on your day and actions
4. Face your shortcomings
5. Ask God for guidance and pray about tomorrow

I'M THANKFUL FOR...

MY SINS & SHORTCOMINGS TODAY

Examen

Day 24   *Morning Prayer*

O Jesus, through the Immaculate Heart of Mary, I offer You my prayers, works, joys and sufferings of this day for all the intentions of Your Sacred Heart, in union with the Holy Sacrifice of the Mass throughout the world, in reparation for my sins, for the intentions of all my relatives and friends, and in particular for the intentions of the Holy Father. Amen.

READ & WRITE IT: BIBLE VERSE

REFLECT: WHAT DOES THIS MEAN TO ME?

RESPOND: WHAT DO I SAY TO GOD ABOUT THIS?

REST IN MEDITATION: HOW IS GOD ASKING ME TO CHANGE?

Lectio Devina

1. Ask God to see your day and actions through His eyes
2. Thank Him
3. Review and meditate on your day and actions
4. Face your shortcomings
5. Ask God for guidance and pray about tomorrow

I'M THANKFUL FOR...

MY SINS & SHORTCOMINGS TODAY

Examen

Day 25

O Jesus, through the Immaculate Heart of Mary, I offer You my prayers, works, joys and sufferings of this day for all the intentions of Your Sacred Heart, in union with the Holy Sacrifice of the Mass throughout the world, in reparation for my sins, for the intentions of all my relatives and friends, and in particular for the intentions of the Holy Father. Amen.

READ & WRITE IT OUT: BIBLE VERSE

REFLECT: WHAT DOES THIS MEAN TO ME?

RESPOND: WHAT DO I SAY TO GOD ABOUT THIS?

REST IN MEDITATION: HOW IS GOD ASKING ME TO CHANGE?

Lectio Devina

| 1. Ask God to see your day and actions through His eyes 2. Thank Him 3. Review and meditate on your day and actions 4. Face your shortcomings 5. Ask God for guidance and pray about tomorrow | I'M THANKFUL FOR... | MY SINS & SHORTCOMINGS TODAY |

Examen

Day 26

Morning Prayer

O Jesus, through the Immaculate Heart of Mary, I offer You my prayers, works, joys and sufferings of this day for all the intentions of Your Sacred Heart, in union with the Holy Sacrifice of the Mass throughout the world, in reparation for my sins, for the intentions of all my relatives and friends, and in particular for the intentions of the Holy Father. Amen.

READ & WRITE IT: BIBLE VERSE

REFLECT: WHAT DOES THIS MEAN TO ME?

RESPOND: WHAT DO I SAY TO GOD ABOUT THIS?

REST IN MEDITATION: HOW IS GOD ASKING ME TO CHANGE?

Lectio Devina

| 1. Ask God to see your day and actions through His eyes 2. Thank Him 3. Review and meditate on your day and actions 4. Face your shortcomings 5. Ask God for guidance and pray about tomorrow | I'M THANKFUL FOR... | MY SINS & SHORTCOMINGS TODAY |

Examen

Day 27   *Morning Prayer*

O Jesus, through the Immaculate Heart of Mary, I offer You my prayers, works, joys and sufferings of this day for all the intentions of Your Sacred Heart, in union with the Holy Sacrifice of the Mass throughout the world, in reparation for my sins, for the intentions of all my relatives and friends, and in particular for the intentions of the Holy Father. Amen.

Lectio Devina

READ & WRITE IT OUT: BIBLE VERSE

REFLECT: WHAT DOES THIS MEAN TO ME?

RESPOND: WHAT DO I SAY TO GOD ABOUT THIS?

REST IN MEDITATION: HOW IS GOD ASKING ME TO CHANGE?

Examen

1. Ask God to see your day and actions through His eyes
2. Thank Him
3. Review and meditate on your day and actions
4. Face your shortcomings
5. Ask God for guidance and pray about tomorrow

I'M THANKFUL FOR...

MY SINS & SHORTCOMINGS TODAY

Day 28   *Morning Prayer*

O Jesus, through the Immaculate Heart of Mary, I offer You my prayers, works, joys and sufferings of this day for all the intentions of Your Sacred Heart, in union with the Holy Sacrifice of the Mass throughout the world, in reparation for my sins, for the intentions of all my relatives and friends, and in particular for the intentions of the Holy Father. Amen.

Lectio Devina

READ & WRITE IT: BIBLE VERSE

REFLECT: WHAT DOES THIS MEAN TO ME?

RESPOND: WHAT DO I SAY TO GOD ABOUT THIS?

REST IN MEDITATION: HOW IS GOD ASKING ME TO CHANGE?

Examen

1. Ask God to see your day and actions through His eyes
2. Thank Him
3. Review and meditate on your day and actions
4. Face your shortcomings
5. Ask God for guidance and pray about tomorrow

I'M THANKFUL FOR...

MY SINS & SHORTCOMINGS TODAY

Day 29

Morning Prayer

O Jesus, through the Immaculate Heart of Mary, I offer You my prayers, works, joys and sufferings of this day for all the intentions of Your Sacred Heart, in union with the Holy Sacrifice of the Mass throughout the world, in reparation for my sins, for the intentions of all my relatives and friends, and in particular for the intentions of the Holy Father. Amen.

Lectio Devina

READ & WRITE IT OUT: BIBLE VERSE

REFLECT: WHAT DOES THIS MEAN TO ME?

RESPOND: WHAT DO I SAY TO GOD ABOUT THIS?

REST IN MEDITATION: HOW IS GOD ASKING ME TO CHANGE?

Examen

1. Ask God to see your day and actions through His eyes
2. Thank Him
3. Review and meditate on your day and actions
4. Face your shortcomings
5. Ask God for guidance and pray about tomorrow

I'M THANKFUL FOR...

MY SINS & SHORTCOMINGS TODAY

Day 30

Morning Prayer

O Jesus, through the Immaculate Heart of Mary, I offer You my prayers, works, joys and sufferings of this day for all the intentions of Your Sacred Heart, in union with the Holy Sacrifice of the Mass throughout the world, in reparation for my sins, for the intentions of all my relatives and friends, and in particular for the intentions of the Holy Father. Amen.

Lectio Devina

READ & WRITE IT: BIBLE VERSE

REFLECT: WHAT DOES THIS MEAN TO ME?

RESPOND: WHAT DO I SAY TO GOD ABOUT THIS?

REST IN MEDITATION: HOW IS GOD ASKING ME TO CHANGE?

Examen

1. Ask God to see your day and actions through His eyes
2. Thank Him
3. Review and meditate on your day and actions
4. Face your shortcomings
5. Ask God for guidance and pray about tomorrow

I'M THANKFUL FOR...

MY SINS & SHORTCOMINGS TODAY

Day 31   *Morning Prayer*

O Jesus, through the Immaculate Heart of Mary, I offer You my prayers, works, joys and sufferings of this day for all the intentions of Your Sacred Heart, in union with the Holy Sacrifice of the Mass throughout the world, in reparation for my sins, for the intentions of all my relatives and friends, and in particular for the intentions of the Holy Father. Amen.

READ & WRITE IT OUT: BIBLE VERSE

REFLECT: WHAT DOES THIS MEAN TO ME?

RESPOND: WHAT DO I SAY TO GOD ABOUT THIS?

REST IN MEDITATION: HOW IS GOD ASKING ME TO CHANGE?

Lectio Devina

1. Ask God to see your day and actions through His eyes
2. Thank Him
3. Review and meditate on your day and actions
4. Face your shortcomings
5. Ask God for guidance and pray about tomorrow

Examen

I'M THANKFUL FOR...

MY SINS & SHORTCOMINGS TODAY

PRAYERS & REFLECTIONS ON YOUR SPIRITUAL JOURNEY THIS MONTH

November

Eternal Father, I offer You the most precious blood of thy Divine Son, Jesus, in union with the Masses said throughout the world today, for all the Holy Souls in Purgatory, for sinners everywhere, for sinners in the universal Church, for those in my own home, and in my family. Amen (St. Gertrude the Great Prayer)

PERSONAL RESOLUTIONS

SPIRITUAL READING LOG

LAST CONFESSION DATE

HOLY ACTIVITIES WITH MY FAMILY/ FRIENDS

PRAYER REQUESTS

ROSARY & CHAPLET TRACKER

"We are all called to be great saints; don't miss the opportunity!" - Mother Angelica

Day 1

Morning Prayer

O Jesus, through the Immaculate Heart of Mary, I offer You my prayers, works, joys and sufferings of this day for all the intentions of Your Sacred Heart, in union with the Holy Sacrifice of the Mass throughout the world, in reparation for my sins, for the intentions of all my relatives and friends, and in particular for the intentions of the Holy Father. Amen.

Lectio Devina

READ & WRITE IT OUT: BIBLE VERSE

REFLECT: WHAT DOES THIS MEAN TO ME?

RESPOND: WHAT DO I SAY TO GOD ABOUT THIS?

REST IN MEDITATION: HOW IS GOD ASKING ME TO CHANGE?

Examen

1. Ask God to see your day and actions through His eyes
2. Thank Him
3. Review and meditate on your day and actions
4. Face your shortcomings
5. Ask God for guidance and pray about tomorrow

I'M THANKFUL FOR...

MY SINS & SHORTCOMINGS TODAY

Day 2

Morning Prayer

O Jesus, through the Immaculate Heart of Mary, I offer You my prayers, works, joys and sufferings of this day for all the intentions of Your Sacred Heart, in union with the Holy Sacrifice of the Mass throughout the world, in reparation for my sins, for the intentions of all my relatives and friends, and in particular for the intentions of the Holy Father. Amen.

Lectio Devina

READ & WRITE IT: BIBLE VERSE

REFLECT: WHAT DOES THIS MEAN TO ME?

RESPOND: WHAT DO I SAY TO GOD ABOUT THIS?

REST IN MEDITATION: HOW IS GOD ASKING ME TO CHANGE?

Examen

1. Ask God to see your day and actions through His eyes
2. Thank Him
3. Review and meditate on your day and actions
4. Face your shortcomings
5. Ask God for guidance and pray about tomorrow

I'M THANKFUL FOR...

MY SINS & SHORTCOMINGS TODAY

Day 3

Morning Prayer

O Jesus, through the Immaculate Heart of Mary, I offer You my prayers, works, joys and sufferings of this day for all the intentions of Your Sacred Heart, in union with the Holy Sacrifice of the Mass throughout the world, in reparation for my sins, for the intentions of all my relatives and friends, and in particular for the intentions of the Holy Father. Amen.

Lectio Devina

READ & WRITE IT OUT: BIBLE VERSE

REFLECT: WHAT DOES THIS MEAN TO ME?

RESPOND: WHAT DO I SAY TO GOD ABOUT THIS?

REST IN MEDITATION: HOW IS GOD ASKING ME TO CHANGE?

Examen

1. Ask God to see your day and actions through His eyes
2. Thank Him
3. Review and meditate on your day and actions
4. Face your shortcomings
5. Ask God for guidance and pray about tomorrow

I'M THANKFUL FOR...

MY SINS & SHORTCOMINGS TODAY

Day 4

Morning Prayer

O Jesus, through the Immaculate Heart of Mary, I offer You my prayers, works, joys and sufferings of this day for all the intentions of Your Sacred Heart, in union with the Holy Sacrifice of the Mass throughout the world, in reparation for my sins, for the intentions of all my relatives and friends, and in particular for the intentions of the Holy Father. Amen.

Lectio Devina

READ & WRITE IT: BIBLE VERSE

REFLECT: WHAT DOES THIS MEAN TO ME?

RESPOND: WHAT DO I SAY TO GOD ABOUT THIS?

REST IN MEDITATION: HOW IS GOD ASKING ME TO CHANGE?

Examen

1. Ask God to see your day and actions through His eyes
2. Thank Him
3. Review and meditate on your day and actions
4. Face your shortcomings
5. Ask God for guidance and pray about tomorrow

I'M THANKFUL FOR...

MY SINS & SHORTCOMINGS TODAY

Day 5

Morning Prayer

O Jesus, through the Immaculate Heart of Mary, I offer You my prayers, works, joys and sufferings of this day for all the intentions of Your Sacred Heart, in union with the Holy Sacrifice of the Mass throughout the world, in reparation for my sins, for the intentions of all my relatives and friends, and in particular for the intentions of the Holy Father. Amen.

Lectio Devina

READ & WRITE IT OUT: BIBLE VERSE

REFLECT: WHAT DOES THIS MEAN TO ME?

RESPOND: WHAT DO I SAY TO GOD ABOUT THIS?

REST IN MEDITATION: HOW IS GOD ASKING ME TO CHANGE?

Examen

1. Ask God to see your day and actions through His eyes
2. Thank Him
3. Review and meditate on your day and actions
4. Face your shortcomings
5. Ask God for guidance and pray about tomorrow

I'M THANKFUL FOR...

MY SINS & SHORTCOMINGS TODAY

Day 6

Morning Prayer

O Jesus, through the Immaculate Heart of Mary, I offer You my prayers, works, joys and sufferings of this day for all the intentions of Your Sacred Heart, in union with the Holy Sacrifice of the Mass throughout the world, in reparation for my sins, for the intentions of all my relatives and friends, and in particular for the intentions of the Holy Father. Amen.

Lectio Devina

READ & WRITE IT: BIBLE VERSE

REFLECT: WHAT DOES THIS MEAN TO ME?

RESPOND: WHAT DO I SAY TO GOD ABOUT THIS?

REST IN MEDITATION: HOW IS GOD ASKING ME TO CHANGE?

Examen

1. Ask God to see your day and actions through His eyes
2. Thank Him
3. Review and meditate on your day and actions
4. Face your shortcomings
5. Ask God for guidance and pray about tomorrow

I'M THANKFUL FOR...

MY SINS & SHORTCOMINGS TODAY

Day 7

O Jesus, through the Immaculate Heart of Mary, I offer You my prayers, works, joys and sufferings of this day for all the intentions of Your Sacred Heart, in union with the Holy Sacrifice of the Mass throughout the world, in reparation for my sins, for the intentions of all my relatives and friends, and in particular for the intentions of the Holy Father. Amen.

READ & WRITE IT OUT: BIBLE VERSE

REFLECT: WHAT DOES THIS MEAN TO ME?

RESPOND: WHAT DO I SAY TO GOD ABOUT THIS?

REST IN MEDITATION: HOW IS GOD ASKING ME TO CHANGE?

Lectio Devina

1. Ask God to see your day and actions through His eyes
2. Thank Him
3. Review and meditate on your day and actions
4. Face your shortcomings
5. Ask God for guidance and pray about tomorrow

I'M THANKFUL FOR...

MY SINS & SHORTCOMINGS TODAY

Examen

Day 8

Morning Prayer

O Jesus, through the Immaculate Heart of Mary, I offer You my prayers, works, joys and sufferings of this day for all the intentions of Your Sacred Heart, in union with the Holy Sacrifice of the Mass throughout the world, in reparation for my sins, for the intentions of all my relatives and friends, and in particular for the intentions of the Holy Father. Amen.

READ & WRITE IT: BIBLE VERSE

REFLECT: WHAT DOES THIS MEAN TO ME?

RESPOND: WHAT DO I SAY TO GOD ABOUT THIS?

REST IN MEDITATION: HOW IS GOD ASKING ME TO CHANGE?

Lectio Devina

1. Ask God to see your day and actions through His eyes
2. Thank Him
3. Review and meditate on your day and actions
4. Face your shortcomings
5. Ask God for guidance and pray about tomorrow

I'M THANKFUL FOR...

MY SINS & SHORTCOMINGS TODAY

Examen

Day 9

Morning Prayer

O Jesus, through the Immaculate Heart of Mary, I offer You my prayers, works, joys and sufferings of this day for all the intentions of Your Sacred Heart, in union with the Holy Sacrifice of the Mass throughout the world, in reparation for my sins, for the intentions of all my relatives and friends, and in particular for the intentions of the Holy Father. Amen.

Lectio Devina

READ & WRITE IT OUT: BIBLE VERSE

REFLECT: WHAT DOES THIS MEAN TO ME?

RESPOND: WHAT DO I SAY TO GOD ABOUT THIS?

REST IN MEDITATION: HOW IS GOD ASKING ME TO CHANGE?

Examen

1. Ask God to see your day and actions through His eyes
2. Thank Him
3. Review and meditate on your day and actions
4. Face your shortcomings
5. Ask God for guidance and pray about tomorrow

I'M THANKFUL FOR...

MY SINS & SHORTCOMINGS TODAY

Day 10

Morning Prayer

O Jesus, through the Immaculate Heart of Mary, I offer You my prayers, works, joys and sufferings of this day for all the intentions of Your Sacred Heart, in union with the Holy Sacrifice of the Mass throughout the world, in reparation for my sins, for the intentions of all my relatives and friends, and in particular for the intentions of the Holy Father. Amen.

Lectio Devina

READ & WRITE IT: BIBLE VERSE

REFLECT: WHAT DOES THIS MEAN TO ME?

RESPOND: WHAT DO I SAY TO GOD ABOUT THIS?

REST IN MEDITATION: HOW IS GOD ASKING ME TO CHANGE?

Examen

1. Ask God to see your day and actions through His eyes
2. Thank Him
3. Review and meditate on your day and actions
4. Face your shortcomings
5. Ask God for guidance and pray about tomorrow

I'M THANKFUL FOR...

MY SINS & SHORTCOMINGS TODAY

Day 11

Morning Prayer

O Jesus, through the Immaculate Heart of Mary, I offer You my prayers, works, joys and sufferings of this day for all the intentions of Your Sacred Heart, in union with the Holy Sacrifice of the Mass throughout the world, in reparation for my sins, for the intentions of all my relatives and friends, and in particular for the intentions of the Holy Father. Amen.

READ & WRITE IT OUT: BIBLE VERSE

REFLECT: WHAT DOES THIS MEAN TO ME?

RESPOND: WHAT DO I SAY TO GOD ABOUT THIS?

REST IN MEDITATION: HOW IS GOD ASKING ME TO CHANGE?

Lectio Devina

1. Ask God to see your day and actions through His eyes
2. Thank Him
3. Review and meditate on your day and actions
4. Face your shortcomings
5. Ask God for guidance and pray about tomorrow

Examen

I'M THANKFUL FOR...

MY SINS & SHORTCOMINGS TODAY

Day 12

Morning Prayer

O Jesus, through the Immaculate Heart of Mary, I offer You my prayers, works, joys and sufferings of this day for all the intentions of Your Sacred Heart, in union with the Holy Sacrifice of the Mass throughout the world, in reparation for my sins, for the intentions of all my relatives and friends, and in particular for the intentions of the Holy Father. Amen.

READ & WRITE IT: BIBLE VERSE

REFLECT: WHAT DOES THIS MEAN TO ME?

RESPOND: WHAT DO I SAY TO GOD ABOUT THIS?

REST IN MEDITATION: HOW IS GOD ASKING ME TO CHANGE?

Lectio Devina

1. Ask God to see your day and actions through His eyes
2. Thank Him
3. Review and meditate on your day and actions
4. Face your shortcomings
5. Ask God for guidance and pray about tomorrow

Examen

I'M THANKFUL FOR...

MY SINS & SHORTCOMINGS TODAY

Day 13

Morning Prayer

O Jesus, through the Immaculate Heart of Mary, I offer You my prayers, works, joys and sufferings of this day for all the intentions of Your Sacred Heart, in union with the Holy Sacrifice of the Mass throughout the world, in reparation for my sins, for the intentions of all my relatives and friends, and in particular for the intentions of the Holy Father. Amen.

Lectio Devina

READ & WRITE IT OUT: BIBLE VERSE

REFLECT: WHAT DOES THIS MEAN TO ME?

RESPOND: WHAT DO I SAY TO GOD ABOUT THIS?

REST IN MEDITATION: HOW IS GOD ASKING ME TO CHANGE?

Examen

1. Ask God to see your day and actions through His eyes
2. Thank Him
3. Review and meditate on your day and actions
4. Face your shortcomings
5. Ask God for guidance and pray about tomorrow

I'M THANKFUL FOR...

MY SINS & SHORTCOMINGS TODAY

Day 14

Morning Prayer

O Jesus, through the Immaculate Heart of Mary, I offer You my prayers, works, joys and sufferings of this day for all the intentions of Your Sacred Heart, in union with the Holy Sacrifice of the Mass throughout the world, in reparation for my sins, for the intentions of all my relatives and friends, and in particular for the intentions of the Holy Father. Amen.

Lectio Devina

READ & WRITE IT: BIBLE VERSE

REFLECT: WHAT DOES THIS MEAN TO ME?

RESPOND: WHAT DO I SAY TO GOD ABOUT THIS?

REST IN MEDITATION: HOW IS GOD ASKING ME TO CHANGE?

Examen

1. Ask God to see your day and actions through His eyes
2. Thank Him
3. Review and meditate on your day and actions
4. Face your shortcomings
5. Ask God for guidance and pray about tomorrow

I'M THANKFUL FOR...

MY SINS & SHORTCOMINGS TODAY

Day 15

O Jesus, through the Immaculate Heart of Mary, I offer You my prayers, works, joys and sufferings of this day for all the intentions of Your Sacred Heart, in union with the Holy Sacrifice of the Mass throughout the world, in reparation for my sins, for the intentions of all my relatives and friends, and in particular for the intentions of the Holy Father. Amen.

Lectio Devina

READ & WRITE IT OUT: BIBLE VERSE

REFLECT: WHAT DOES THIS MEAN TO ME?

RESPOND: WHAT DO I SAY TO GOD ABOUT THIS?

REST IN MEDITATION: HOW IS GOD ASKING ME TO CHANGE?

Examen

1. Ask God to see your day and actions through His eyes
2. Thank Him
3. Review and meditate on your day and actions
4. Face your shortcomings
5. Ask God for guidance and pray about tomorrow

I'M THANKFUL FOR...

MY SINS & SHORTCOMINGS TODAY

Day 16

Morning Prayer

O Jesus, through the Immaculate Heart of Mary, I offer You my prayers, works, joys and sufferings of this day for all the intentions of Your Sacred Heart, in union with the Holy Sacrifice of the Mass throughout the world, in reparation for my sins, for the intentions of all my relatives and friends, and in particular for the intentions of the Holy Father. Amen.

Lectio Devina

READ & WRITE IT: BIBLE VERSE

REFLECT: WHAT DOES THIS MEAN TO ME?

RESPOND: WHAT DO I SAY TO GOD ABOUT THIS?

REST IN MEDITATION: HOW IS GOD ASKING ME TO CHANGE?

Examen

1. Ask God to see your day and actions through His eyes
2. Thank Him
3. Review and meditate on your day and actions
4. Face your shortcomings
5. Ask God for guidance and pray about tomorrow

I'M THANKFUL FOR...

MY SINS & SHORTCOMINGS TODAY

Day 17   *Morning Prayer*

O Jesus, through the Immaculate Heart of Mary, I offer You my prayers, works, joys and sufferings of this day for all the intentions of Your Sacred Heart, in union with the Holy Sacrifice of the Mass throughout the world, in reparation for my sins, for the intentions of all my relatives and friends, and in particular for the intentions of the Holy Father. Amen.

READ & WRITE IT OUT: BIBLE VERSE

REFLECT: WHAT DOES THIS MEAN TO ME?

RESPOND: WHAT DO I SAY TO GOD ABOUT THIS?

REST IN MEDITATION: HOW IS GOD ASKING ME TO CHANGE?

Lectio Devina

1. Ask God to see your day and actions through His eyes
2. Thank Him
3. Review and meditate on your day and actions
4. Face your shortcomings
5. Ask God for guidance and pray about tomorrow

Examen

I'M THANKFUL FOR...

MY SINS & SHORTCOMINGS TODAY

Day 18   *Morning Prayer*

O Jesus, through the Immaculate Heart of Mary, I offer You my prayers, works, joys and sufferings of this day for all the intentions of Your Sacred Heart, in union with the Holy Sacrifice of the Mass throughout the world, in reparation for my sins, for the intentions of all my relatives and friends, and in particular for the intentions of the Holy Father. Amen.

READ & WRITE IT: BIBLE VERSE

REFLECT: WHAT DOES THIS MEAN TO ME?

RESPOND: WHAT DO I SAY TO GOD ABOUT THIS?

REST IN MEDITATION: HOW IS GOD ASKING ME TO CHANGE?

Lectio Devina

1. Ask God to see your day and actions through His eyes
2. Thank Him
3. Review and meditate on your day and actions
4. Face your shortcomings
5. Ask God for guidance and pray about tomorrow

Examen

I'M THANKFUL FOR...

MY SINS & SHORTCOMINGS TODAY

Day 19   *Morning Prayer*

O Jesus, through the Immaculate Heart of Mary, I offer You my prayers, works, joys and sufferings of this day for all the intentions of Your Sacred Heart, in union with the Holy Sacrifice of the Mass throughout the world, in reparation for my sins, for the intentions of all my relatives and friends, and in particular for the intentions of the Holy Father. Amen.

READ & WRITE IT OUT: BIBLE VERSE

Lectio Devina

REFLECT: WHAT DOES THIS MEAN TO ME?

RESPOND: WHAT DO I SAY TO GOD ABOUT THIS?

REST IN MEDITATION: HOW IS GOD ASKING ME TO CHANGE?

Examen

1. Ask God to see your day and actions through His eyes
2. Thank Him
3. Review and meditate on your day and actions
4. Face your shortcomings
5. Ask God for guidance and pray about tomorrow

I'M THANKFUL FOR...

MY SINS & SHORTCOMINGS TODAY

Day 20   *Morning Prayer*

O Jesus, through the Immaculate Heart of Mary, I offer You my prayers, works, joys and sufferings of this day for all the intentions of Your Sacred Heart, in union with the Holy Sacrifice of the Mass throughout the world, in reparation for my sins, for the intentions of all my relatives and friends, and in particular for the intentions of the Holy Father. Amen.

READ & WRITE IT: BIBLE VERSE

Lectio Devina

REFLECT: WHAT DOES THIS MEAN TO ME?

RESPOND: WHAT DO I SAY TO GOD ABOUT THIS?

REST IN MEDITATION: HOW IS GOD ASKING ME TO CHANGE?

Examen

1. Ask God to see your day and actions through His eyes
2. Thank Him
3. Review and meditate on your day and actions
4. Face your shortcomings
5. Ask God for guidance and pray about tomorrow

I'M THANKFUL FOR...

MY SINS & SHORTCOMINGS TODAY

Day 21   *Morning Prayer*

O Jesus, through the Immaculate Heart of Mary, I offer You my prayers, works, joys and sufferings of this day for all the intentions of Your Sacred Heart, in union with the Holy Sacrifice of the Mass throughout the world, in reparation for my sins, for the intentions of all my relatives and friends, and in particular for the intentions of the Holy Father. Amen.

Lectio Devina

READ & WRITE IT OUT: BIBLE VERSE

REFLECT: WHAT DOES THIS MEAN TO ME?

RESPOND: WHAT DO I SAY TO GOD ABOUT THIS?

REST IN MEDITATION: HOW IS GOD ASKING ME TO CHANGE?

Examen

1. Ask God to see your day and actions through His eyes
2. Thank Him
3. Review and meditate on your day and actions
4. Face your shortcomings
5. Ask God for guidance and pray about tomorrow

I'M THANKFUL FOR...

MY SINS & SHORTCOMINGS TODAY

Day 22   *Morning Prayer*

O Jesus, through the Immaculate Heart of Mary, I offer You my prayers, works, joys and sufferings of this day for all the intentions of Your Sacred Heart, in union with the Holy Sacrifice of the Mass throughout the world, in reparation for my sins, for the intentions of all my relatives and friends, and in particular for the intentions of the Holy Father. Amen.

Lectio Devina

READ & WRITE IT: BIBLE VERSE

REFLECT: WHAT DOES THIS MEAN TO ME?

RESPOND: WHAT DO I SAY TO GOD ABOUT THIS?

REST IN MEDITATION: HOW IS GOD ASKING ME TO CHANGE?

Examen

1. Ask God to see your day and actions through His eyes
2. Thank Him
3. Review and meditate on your day and actions
4. Face your shortcomings
5. Ask God for guidance and pray about tomorrow

I'M THANKFUL FOR...

MY SINS & SHORTCOMINGS TODAY

Day 23

Morning Prayer

Morning Prayer

O Jesus, through the Immaculate Heart of Mary, I offer You my prayers, works, joys and sufferings of this day for all the intentions of Your Sacred Heart, in union with the Holy Sacrifice of the Mass throughout the world, in reparation for my sins, for the intentions of all my relatives and friends, and in particular for the intentions of the Holy Father. Amen.

READ & WRITE IT OUT: BIBLE VERSE

REFLECT: WHAT DOES THIS MEAN TO ME?

RESPOND: WHAT DO I SAY TO GOD ABOUT THIS?

REST IN MEDITATION: HOW IS GOD ASKING ME TO CHANGE?

Lectio Devina

1. Ask God to see your day and actions through His eyes 2. Thank Him 3. Review and meditate on your day and actions 4. Face your shortcomings 5. Ask God for guidance and pray about tomorrow	I'M THANKFUL FOR...	MY SINS & SHORTCOMINGS TODAY

Examen

Day 24

Morning Prayer

O Jesus, through the Immaculate Heart of Mary, I offer You my prayers, works, joys and sufferings of this day for all the intentions of Your Sacred Heart, in union with the Holy Sacrifice of the Mass throughout the world, in reparation for my sins, for the intentions of all my relatives and friends, and in particular for the intentions of the Holy Father. Amen.

READ & WRITE IT: BIBLE VERSE

REFLECT: WHAT DOES THIS MEAN TO ME?

RESPOND: WHAT DO I SAY TO GOD ABOUT THIS?

REST IN MEDITATION: HOW IS GOD ASKING ME TO CHANGE?

Lectio Devina

1. Ask God to see your day and actions through His eyes 2. Thank Him 3. Review and meditate on your day and actions 4. Face your shortcomings 5. Ask God for guidance and pray about tomorrow	I'M THANKFUL FOR...	MY SINS & SHORTCOMINGS TODAY

Examen

Day 25   *Morning Prayer*

O Jesus, through the Immaculate Heart of Mary, I offer You my prayers, works, joys and sufferings of this day for all the intentions of Your Sacred Heart, in union with the Holy Sacrifice of the Mass throughout the world, in reparation for my sins, for the intentions of all my relatives and friends, and in particular for the intentions of the Holy Father. Amen.

READ & WRITE IT OUT: BIBLE VERSE

REFLECT: WHAT DOES THIS MEAN TO ME?

RESPOND: WHAT DO I SAY TO GOD ABOUT THIS?

REST IN MEDITATION: HOW IS GOD ASKING ME TO CHANGE?

Lectio Devina

1. Ask God to see your day and actions through His eyes
2. Thank Him
3. Review and meditate on your day and actions
4. Face your shortcomings
5. Ask God for guidance and pray about tomorrow

I'M THANKFUL FOR...

MY SINS & SHORTCOMINGS TODAY

Examen

Day 26   *Morning Prayer*

O Jesus, through the Immaculate Heart of Mary, I offer You my prayers, works, joys and sufferings of this day for all the intentions of Your Sacred Heart, in union with the Holy Sacrifice of the Mass throughout the world, in reparation for my sins, for the intentions of all my relatives and friends, and in particular for the intentions of the Holy Father. Amen.

READ & WRITE IT: BIBLE VERSE

REFLECT: WHAT DOES THIS MEAN TO ME?

RESPOND: WHAT DO I SAY TO GOD ABOUT THIS?

REST IN MEDITATION: HOW IS GOD ASKING ME TO CHANGE?

Lectio Devina

1. Ask God to see your day and actions through His eyes
2. Thank Him
3. Review and meditate on your day and actions
4. Face your shortcomings
5. Ask God for guidance and pray about tomorrow

I'M THANKFUL FOR...

MY SINS & SHORTCOMINGS TODAY

Examen

Day 27

Morning Prayer

O Jesus, through the Immaculate Heart of Mary, I offer You my prayers, works, joys and sufferings of this day for all the intentions of Your Sacred Heart, in union with the Holy Sacrifice of the Mass throughout the world, in reparation for my sins, for the intentions of all my relatives and friends, and in particular for the intentions of the Holy Father. Amen.

Lectio Devina

READ & WRITE IT OUT: BIBLE VERSE

REFLECT: WHAT DOES THIS MEAN TO ME?

RESPOND: WHAT DO I SAY TO GOD ABOUT THIS?

REST IN MEDITATION: HOW IS GOD ASKING ME TO CHANGE?

Examen

1. Ask God to see your day and actions through His eyes
2. Thank Him
3. Review and meditate on your day and actions
4. Face your shortcomings
5. Ask God for guidance and pray about tomorrow

I'M THANKFUL FOR...

MY SINS & SHORTCOMINGS TODAY

Day 28

Morning Prayer

O Jesus, through the Immaculate Heart of Mary, I offer You my prayers, works, joys and sufferings of this day for all the intentions of Your Sacred Heart, in union with the Holy Sacrifice of the Mass throughout the world, in reparation for my sins, for the intentions of all my relatives and friends, and in particular for the intentions of the Holy Father. Amen.

Lectio Devina

READ & WRITE IT: BIBLE VERSE

REFLECT: WHAT DOES THIS MEAN TO ME?

RESPOND: WHAT DO I SAY TO GOD ABOUT THIS?

REST IN MEDITATION: HOW IS GOD ASKING ME TO CHANGE?

Examen

1. Ask God to see your day and actions through His eyes
2. Thank Him
3. Review and meditate on your day and actions
4. Face your shortcomings
5. Ask God for guidance and pray about tomorrow

I'M THANKFUL FOR...

MY SINS & SHORTCOMINGS TODAY

Day 29   *Morning Prayer*

O Jesus, through the Immaculate Heart of Mary, I offer You my prayers, works, joys and sufferings of this day for all the intentions of Your Sacred Heart, in union with the Holy Sacrifice of the Mass throughout the world, in reparation for my sins, for the intentions of all my relatives and friends, and in particular for the intentions of the Holy Father. Amen.

READ & WRITE IT OUT: BIBLE VERSE

REFLECT: WHAT DOES THIS MEAN TO ME?

RESPOND: WHAT DO I SAY TO GOD ABOUT THIS?

REST IN MEDITATION: HOW IS GOD ASKING ME TO CHANGE?

Lectio Devina

1. Ask God to see your day and actions through His eyes
2. Thank Him
3. Review and meditate on your day and actions
4. Face your shortcomings
5. Ask God for guidance and pray about tomorrow

I'M THANKFUL FOR...

MY SINS & SHORTCOMINGS TODAY

Examen

Day 30   *Morning Prayer*

O Jesus, through the Immaculate Heart of Mary, I offer You my prayers, works, joys and sufferings of this day for all the intentions of Your Sacred Heart, in union with the Holy Sacrifice of the Mass throughout the world, in reparation for my sins, for the intentions of all my relatives and friends, and in particular for the intentions of the Holy Father. Amen.

READ & WRITE IT: BIBLE VERSE

REFLECT: WHAT DOES THIS MEAN TO ME?

RESPOND: WHAT DO I SAY TO GOD ABOUT THIS?

REST IN MEDITATION: HOW IS GOD ASKING ME TO CHANGE?

Lectio Devina

1. Ask God to see your day and actions through His eyes
2. Thank Him
3. Review and meditate on your day and actions
4. Face your shortcomings
5. Ask God for guidance and pray about tomorrow

I'M THANKFUL FOR...

MY SINS & SHORTCOMINGS TODAY

Examen

PRAYERS & REFLECTIONS ON YOUR SPIRITUAL JOURNEY THIS MONTH

Jesus, I trust in You!

December

Hail and blessed be the hour and moment in which the Son of God was born of the most pure Virgin Mary, at midnight, in Bethlehem, in the piercing cold.
In that hour vouchsafe, O my God, to hear my prayer and grant my desires, through the merits of Our Savior Jesus Christ, and of His blessed Mother.
Amen. (The Saint Andrew Prayer)

PERSONAL RESOLUTIONS

SPIRITUAL READING LOG

LAST CONFESSION DATE

HOLY ACTIVITIES WITH MY FAMILY/ FRIENDS

PRAYER REQUESTS

ROSARY & CHAPLET TRACKER

"We are all called to be great saints; don't miss the opportunity!" - Mother Angelica

Day 1   *Morning Prayer*

O Jesus, through the Immaculate Heart of Mary, I offer You my prayers, works, joys and sufferings of this day for all the intentions of Your Sacred Heart, in union with the Holy Sacrifice of the Mass throughout the world, in reparation for my sins, for the intentions of all my relatives and friends, and in particular for the intentions of the Holy Father. Amen.

READ & WRITE IT OUT: BIBLE VERSE

REFLECT: WHAT DOES THIS MEAN TO ME?

RESPOND: WHAT DO I SAY TO GOD ABOUT THIS?

REST IN MEDITATION: HOW IS GOD ASKING ME TO CHANGE?

1. Ask God to see your day and actions through His eyes
2. Thank Him
3. Review and meditate on your day and actions
4. Face your shortcomings
5. Ask God for guidance and pray about tomorrow

I'M THANKFUL FOR...   MY SINS & SHORTCOMINGS TODAY

Day 2   *Morning Prayer*

O Jesus, through the Immaculate Heart of Mary, I offer You my prayers, works, joys and sufferings of this day for all the intentions of Your Sacred Heart, in union with the Holy Sacrifice of the Mass throughout the world, in reparation for my sins, for the intentions of all my relatives and friends, and in particular for the intentions of the Holy Father. Amen.

READ & WRITE IT: BIBLE VERSE

REFLECT: WHAT DOES THIS MEAN TO ME?

RESPOND: WHAT DO I SAY TO GOD ABOUT THIS?

REST IN MEDITATION: HOW IS GOD ASKING ME TO CHANGE?

1. Ask God to see your day and actions through His eyes
2. Thank Him
3. Review and meditate on your day and actions
4. Face your shortcomings
5. Ask God for guidance and pray about tomorrow

I'M THANKFUL FOR...   MY SINS & SHORTCOMINGS TODAY

Day 3   *Morning Prayer*

O Jesus, through the Immaculate Heart of Mary, I offer You my prayers, works, joys and sufferings of this day for all the intentions of Your Sacred Heart, in union with the Holy Sacrifice of the Mass throughout the world, in reparation for my sins, for the intentions of all my relatives and friends, and in particular for the intentions of the Holy Father. Amen.

READ & WRITE IT OUT: BIBLE VERSE

REFLECT: WHAT DOES THIS MEAN TO ME?

RESPOND: WHAT DO I SAY TO GOD ABOUT THIS?

REST IN MEDITATION: HOW IS GOD ASKING ME TO CHANGE?

Lectio Devina

1. Ask God to see your day and actions through His eyes
2. Thank Him
3. Review and meditate on your day and actions
4. Face your shortcomings
5. Ask God for guidance and pray about tomorrow

I'M THANKFUL FOR...

MY SINS & SHORTCOMINGS TODAY

Examen

Day 4   *Morning Prayer*

O Jesus, through the Immaculate Heart of Mary, I offer You my prayers, works, joys and sufferings of this day for all the intentions of Your Sacred Heart, in union with the Holy Sacrifice of the Mass throughout the world, in reparation for my sins, for the intentions of all my relatives and friends, and in particular for the intentions of the Holy Father. Amen.

READ & WRITE IT: BIBLE VERSE

REFLECT: WHAT DOES THIS MEAN TO ME?

RESPOND: WHAT DO I SAY TO GOD ABOUT THIS?

REST IN MEDITATION: HOW IS GOD ASKING ME TO CHANGE?

Lectio Devina

1. Ask God to see your day and actions through His eyes
2. Thank Him
3. Review and meditate on your day and actions
4. Face your shortcomings
5. Ask God for guidance and pray about tomorrow

I'M THANKFUL FOR...

MY SINS & SHORTCOMINGS TODAY

Examen

Day 5

Morning Prayer

Morning Prayer

O Jesus, through the Immaculate Heart of Mary, I offer You my prayers, works, joys and sufferings of this day for all the intentions of Your Sacred Heart, in union with the Holy Sacrifice of the Mass throughout the world, in reparation for my sins, for the intentions of all my relatives and friends, and in particular for the intentions of the Holy Father. Amen.

READ & WRITE IT OUT: BIBLE VERSE

REFLECT: WHAT DOES THIS MEAN TO ME?

RESPOND: WHAT DO I SAY TO GOD ABOUT THIS?

REST IN MEDITATION: HOW IS GOD ASKING ME TO CHANGE?

Lectio Devina

1. Ask God to see your day and actions through His eyes
2. Thank Him
3. Review and meditate on your day and actions
4. Face your shortcomings
5. Ask God for guidance and pray about tomorrow

I'M THANKFUL FOR...

MY SINS & SHORTCOMINGS TODAY

Examen

Day 6

Morning Prayer

O Jesus, through the Immaculate Heart of Mary, I offer You my prayers, works, joys and sufferings of this day for all the intentions of Your Sacred Heart, in union with the Holy Sacrifice of the Mass throughout the world, in reparation for my sins, for the intentions of all my relatives and friends, and in particular for the intentions of the Holy Father. Amen.

READ & WRITE IT: BIBLE VERSE

REFLECT: WHAT DOES THIS MEAN TO ME?

RESPOND: WHAT DO I SAY TO GOD ABOUT THIS?

REST IN MEDITATION: HOW IS GOD ASKING ME TO CHANGE?

Lectio Devina

1. Ask God to see your day and actions through His eyes
2. Thank Him
3. Review and meditate on your day and actions
4. Face your shortcomings
5. Ask God for guidance and pray about tomorrow

I'M THANKFUL FOR...

MY SINS & SHORTCOMINGS TODAY

Examen

Day 7   *Morning Prayer*

O Jesus, through the Immaculate Heart of Mary, I offer You my prayers, works, joys and sufferings of this day for all the intentions of Your Sacred Heart, in union with the Holy Sacrifice of the Mass throughout the world, in reparation for my sins, for the intentions of all my relatives and friends, and in particular for the intentions of the Holy Father. Amen.

READ & WRITE IT OUT: BIBLE VERSE

Lectio Devina

REFLECT: WHAT DOES THIS MEAN TO ME?

RESPOND: WHAT DO I SAY TO GOD ABOUT THIS?

REST IN MEDITATION: HOW IS GOD ASKING ME TO CHANGE?

Examen

1. Ask God to see your day and actions through His eyes
2. Thank Him
3. Review and meditate on your day and actions
4. Face your shortcomings
5. Ask God for guidance and pray about tomorrow

I'M THANKFUL FOR...   MY SINS & SHORTCOMINGS TODAY

Day 8   *Morning Prayer*

O Jesus, through the Immaculate Heart of Mary, I offer You my prayers, works, joys and sufferings of this day for all the intentions of Your Sacred Heart, in union with the Holy Sacrifice of the Mass throughout the world, in reparation for my sins, for the intentions of all my relatives and friends, and in particular for the intentions of the Holy Father. Amen.

READ & WRITE IT: BIBLE VERSE

Lectio Devina

REFLECT: WHAT DOES THIS MEAN TO ME?

RESPOND: WHAT DO I SAY TO GOD ABOUT THIS?

REST IN MEDITATION: HOW IS GOD ASKING ME TO CHANGE?

Examen

1. Ask God to see your day and actions through His eyes
2. Thank Him
3. Review and meditate on your day and actions
4. Face your shortcomings
5. Ask God for guidance and pray about tomorrow

I'M THANKFUL FOR...   MY SINS & SHORTCOMINGS TODAY

Day 9

O Jesus, through the Immaculate Heart of Mary, I offer You my prayers, works, joys and sufferings of this day for all the intentions of Your Sacred Heart, in union with the Holy Sacrifice of the Mass throughout the world, in reparation for my sins, for the intentions of all my relatives and friends, and in particular for the intentions of the Holy Father. Amen.

Lectio Devina

READ & WRITE IT OUT: BIBLE VERSE

REFLECT: WHAT DOES THIS MEAN TO ME?

RESPOND: WHAT DO I SAY TO GOD ABOUT THIS?

REST IN MEDITATION: HOW IS GOD ASKING ME TO CHANGE?

Examen

1. Ask God to see your day and actions through His eyes
2. Thank Him
3. Review and meditate on your day and actions
4. Face your shortcomings
5. Ask God for guidance and pray about tomorrow

I'M THANKFUL FOR...

MY SINS & SHORTCOMINGS TODAY

Day 10

Morning Prayer

O Jesus, through the Immaculate Heart of Mary, I offer You my prayers, works, joys and sufferings of this day for all the intentions of Your Sacred Heart, in union with the Holy Sacrifice of the Mass throughout the world, in reparation for my sins, for the intentions of all my relatives and friends, and in particular for the intentions of the Holy Father. Amen.

Lectio Devina

READ & WRITE IT: BIBLE VERSE

REFLECT: WHAT DOES THIS MEAN TO ME?

RESPOND: WHAT DO I SAY TO GOD ABOUT THIS?

REST IN MEDITATION: HOW IS GOD ASKING ME TO CHANGE?

Examen

1. Ask God to see your day and actions through His eyes
2. Thank Him
3. Review and meditate on your day and actions
4. Face your shortcomings
5. Ask God for guidance and pray about tomorrow

I'M THANKFUL FOR...

MY SINS & SHORTCOMINGS TODAY

Day 11   *Morning Prayer*

O Jesus, through the Immaculate Heart of Mary, I offer You my prayers, works, joys and sufferings of this day for all the intentions of Your Sacred Heart, in union with the Holy Sacrifice of the Mass throughout the world, in reparation for my sins, for the intentions of all my relatives and friends, and in particular for the intentions of the Holy Father. Amen.

Lectio Devina

READ & WRITE IT OUT: BIBLE VERSE

REFLECT: WHAT DOES THIS MEAN TO ME?

RESPOND: WHAT DO I SAY TO GOD ABOUT THIS?

REST IN MEDITATION: HOW IS GOD ASKING ME TO CHANGE?

Examen

1. Ask God to see your day and actions through His eyes
2. Thank Him
3. Review and meditate on your day and actions
4. Face your shortcomings
5. Ask God for guidance and pray about tomorrow

I'M THANKFUL FOR...

MY SINS & SHORTCOMINGS TODAY

Day 12   *Morning Prayer*

O Jesus, through the Immaculate Heart of Mary, I offer You my prayers, works, joys and sufferings of this day for all the intentions of Your Sacred Heart, in union with the Holy Sacrifice of the Mass throughout the world, in reparation for my sins, for the intentions of all my relatives and friends, and in particular for the intentions of the Holy Father. Amen.

Lectio Devina

READ & WRITE IT: BIBLE VERSE

REFLECT: WHAT DOES THIS MEAN TO ME?

RESPOND: WHAT DO I SAY TO GOD ABOUT THIS?

REST IN MEDITATION: HOW IS GOD ASKING ME TO CHANGE?

Examen

1. Ask God to see your day and actions through His eyes
2. Thank Him
3. Review and meditate on your day and actions
4. Face your shortcomings
5. Ask God for guidance and pray about tomorrow

I'M THANKFUL FOR...

MY SINS & SHORTCOMINGS TODAY

Day 13   *Morning Prayer*

O Jesus, through the Immaculate Heart of Mary, I offer You my prayers, works, joys and sufferings of this day for all the intentions of Your Sacred Heart, in union with the Holy Sacrifice of the Mass throughout the world, in reparation for my sins, for the intentions of all my relatives and friends, and in particular for the intentions of the Holy Father. Amen.

READ & WRITE IT OUT: BIBLE VERSE

REFLECT: WHAT DOES THIS MEAN TO ME?

RESPOND: WHAT DO I SAY TO GOD ABOUT THIS?

REST IN MEDITATION: HOW IS GOD ASKING ME TO CHANGE?

Lectio Devina

1. Ask God to see your day and actions through His eyes
2. Thank Him
3. Review and meditate on your day and actions
4. Face your shortcomings
5. Ask God for guidance and pray about tomorrow

Examen

I'M THANKFUL FOR...   MY SINS & SHORTCOMINGS TODAY

Day 14   *Morning Prayer*

O Jesus, through the Immaculate Heart of Mary, I offer You my prayers, works, joys and sufferings of this day for all the intentions of Your Sacred Heart, in union with the Holy Sacrifice of the Mass throughout the world, in reparation for my sins, for the intentions of all my relatives and friends, and in particular for the intentions of the Holy Father. Amen.

READ & WRITE IT: BIBLE VERSE

REFLECT: WHAT DOES THIS MEAN TO ME?

RESPOND: WHAT DO I SAY TO GOD ABOUT THIS?

REST IN MEDITATION: HOW IS GOD ASKING ME TO CHANGE?

Lectio Devina

1. Ask God to see your day and actions through His eyes
2. Thank Him
3. Review and meditate on your day and actions
4. Face your shortcomings
5. Ask God for guidance and pray about tomorrow

Examen

I'M THANKFUL FOR...   MY SINS & SHORTCOMINGS TODAY

Day 15

Morning Prayer

O Jesus, through the Immaculate Heart of Mary, I offer You my prayers, works, joys and sufferings of this day for all the intentions of Your Sacred Heart, in union with the Holy Sacrifice of the Mass throughout the world, in reparation for my sins, for the intentions of all my relatives and friends, and in particular for the intentions of the Holy Father. Amen.

Lectio Devina

READ & WRITE IT OUT: BIBLE VERSE

REFLECT: WHAT DOES THIS MEAN TO ME?

RESPOND: WHAT DO I SAY TO GOD ABOUT THIS?

REST IN MEDITATION: HOW IS GOD ASKING ME TO CHANGE?

Examen

1. Ask God to see your day and actions through His eyes
2. Thank Him
3. Review and meditate on your day and actions
4. Face your shortcomings
5. Ask God for guidance and pray about tomorrow

I'M THANKFUL FOR...

MY SINS & SHORTCOMINGS TODAY

Day 16

Morning Prayer

O Jesus, through the Immaculate Heart of Mary, I offer You my prayers, works, joys and sufferings of this day for all the intentions of Your Sacred Heart, in union with the Holy Sacrifice of the Mass throughout the world, in reparation for my sins, for the intentions of all my relatives and friends, and in particular for the intentions of the Holy Father. Amen.

Lectio Devina

READ & WRITE IT: BIBLE VERSE

REFLECT: WHAT DOES THIS MEAN TO ME?

RESPOND: WHAT DO I SAY TO GOD ABOUT THIS?

REST IN MEDITATION: HOW IS GOD ASKING ME TO CHANGE?

Examen

1. Ask God to see your day and actions through His eyes
2. Thank Him
3. Review and meditate on your day and actions
4. Face your shortcomings
5. Ask God for guidance and pray about tomorrow

I'M THANKFUL FOR...

MY SINS & SHORTCOMINGS TODAY

Day 17

O Jesus, through the Immaculate Heart of Mary, I offer You my prayers, works, joys and sufferings of this day for all the intentions of Your Sacred Heart, in union with the Holy Sacrifice of the Mass throughout the world, in reparation for my sins, for the intentions of all my relatives and friends, and in particular for the intentions of the Holy Father. Amen.

Lectio Devina

READ & WRITE IT OUT: BIBLE VERSE

REFLECT: WHAT DOES THIS MEAN TO ME?

RESPOND: WHAT DO I SAY TO GOD ABOUT THIS?

REST IN MEDITATION: HOW IS GOD ASKING ME TO CHANGE?

Examen

1. Ask God to see your day and actions through His eyes
2. Thank Him
3. Review and meditate on your day and actions
4. Face your shortcomings
5. Ask God for guidance and pray about tomorrow

I'M THANKFUL FOR...

MY SINS & SHORTCOMINGS TODAY

Day 18

Morning Prayer

O Jesus, through the Immaculate Heart of Mary, I offer You my prayers, works, joys and sufferings of this day for all the intentions of Your Sacred Heart, in union with the Holy Sacrifice of the Mass throughout the world, in reparation for my sins, for the intentions of all my relatives and friends, and in particular for the intentions of the Holy Father. Amen.

Lectio Devina

READ & WRITE IT: BIBLE VERSE

REFLECT: WHAT DOES THIS MEAN TO ME?

RESPOND: WHAT DO I SAY TO GOD ABOUT THIS?

REST IN MEDITATION: HOW IS GOD ASKING ME TO CHANGE?

Examen

1. Ask God to see your day and actions through His eyes
2. Thank Him
3. Review and meditate on your day and actions
4. Face your shortcomings
5. Ask God for guidance and pray about tomorrow

I'M THANKFUL FOR...

MY SINS & SHORTCOMINGS TODAY

Day 19

O Jesus, through the Immaculate Heart of Mary, I offer You my prayers, works, joys and sufferings of this day for all the intentions of Your Sacred Heart, in union with the Holy Sacrifice of the Mass throughout the world, in reparation for my sins, for the intentions of all my relatives and friends, and in particular for the intentions of the Holy Father. Amen.

Lectio Devina

READ & WRITE IT OUT: BIBLE VERSE

REFLECT: WHAT DOES THIS MEAN TO ME?

RESPOND: WHAT DO I SAY TO GOD ABOUT THIS?

REST IN MEDITATION: HOW IS GOD ASKING ME TO CHANGE?

Examen

1. Ask God to see your day and actions through His eyes
2. Thank Him
3. Review and meditate on your day and actions
4. Face your shortcomings
5. Ask God for guidance and pray about tomorrow

I'M THANKFUL FOR...

MY SINS & SHORTCOMINGS TODAY

Day 20

Morning Prayer

O Jesus, through the Immaculate Heart of Mary, I offer You my prayers, works, joys and sufferings of this day for all the intentions of Your Sacred Heart, in union with the Holy Sacrifice of the Mass throughout the world, in reparation for my sins, for the intentions of all my relatives and friends, and in particular for the intentions of the Holy Father. Amen.

Lectio Devina

READ & WRITE IT: BIBLE VERSE

REFLECT: WHAT DOES THIS MEAN TO ME?

RESPOND: WHAT DO I SAY TO GOD ABOUT THIS?

REST IN MEDITATION: HOW IS GOD ASKING ME TO CHANGE?

Examen

1. Ask God to see your day and actions through His eyes
2. Thank Him
3. Review and meditate on your day and actions
4. Face your shortcomings
5. Ask God for guidance and pray about tomorrow

I'M THANKFUL FOR...

MY SINS & SHORTCOMINGS TODAY

Day 21   *Morning Prayer*

O Jesus, through the Immaculate Heart of Mary, I offer You my prayers, works, joys and sufferings of this day for all the intentions of Your Sacred Heart, in union with the Holy Sacrifice of the Mass throughout the world, in reparation for my sins, for the intentions of all my relatives and friends, and in particular for the intentions of the Holy Father. Amen.

READ & WRITE IT OUT: BIBLE VERSE

REFLECT: WHAT DOES THIS MEAN TO ME?

RESPOND: WHAT DO I SAY TO GOD ABOUT THIS?

REST IN MEDITATION: HOW IS GOD ASKING ME TO CHANGE?

Lectio Devina

1. Ask God to see your day and actions through His eyes
2. Thank Him
3. Review and meditate on your day and actions
4. Face your shortcomings
5. Ask God for guidance and pray about tomorrow

I'M THANKFUL FOR...

MY SINS & SHORTCOMINGS TODAY

Examen

Day 22   *Morning Prayer*

O Jesus, through the Immaculate Heart of Mary, I offer You my prayers, works, joys and sufferings of this day for all the intentions of Your Sacred Heart, in union with the Holy Sacrifice of the Mass throughout the world, in reparation for my sins, for the intentions of all my relatives and friends, and in particular for the intentions of the Holy Father. Amen.

READ & WRITE IT: BIBLE VERSE

REFLECT: WHAT DOES THIS MEAN TO ME?

RESPOND: WHAT DO I SAY TO GOD ABOUT THIS?

REST IN MEDITATION: HOW IS GOD ASKING ME TO CHANGE?

Lectio Devina

1. Ask God to see your day and actions through His eyes
2. Thank Him
3. Review and meditate on your day and actions
4. Face your shortcomings
5. Ask God for guidance and pray about tomorrow

I'M THANKFUL FOR...

MY SINS & SHORTCOMINGS TODAY

Examen

Day 23   *Morning Prayer*

O Jesus, through the Immaculate Heart of Mary, I offer You my prayers, works, joys and sufferings of this day for all the intentions of Your Sacred Heart, in union with the Holy Sacrifice of the Mass throughout the world, in reparation for my sins, for the intentions of all my relatives and friends, and in particular for the intentions of the Holy Father. Amen.

Lectio Devina

READ & WRITE IT OUT: BIBLE VERSE

REFLECT: WHAT DOES THIS MEAN TO ME?

RESPOND: WHAT DO I SAY TO GOD ABOUT THIS?

REST IN MEDITATION: HOW IS GOD ASKING ME TO CHANGE?

Examen

1. Ask God to see your day and actions through His eyes
2. Thank Him
3. Review and meditate on your day and actions
4. Face your shortcomings
5. Ask God for guidance and pray about tomorrow

I'M THANKFUL FOR...

MY SINS & SHORTCOMINGS TODAY

Day 24   *Morning Prayer*

O Jesus, through the Immaculate Heart of Mary, I offer You my prayers, works, joys and sufferings of this day for all the intentions of Your Sacred Heart, in union with the Holy Sacrifice of the Mass throughout the world, in reparation for my sins, for the intentions of all my relatives and friends, and in particular for the intentions of the Holy Father. Amen.

Lectio Devina

READ & WRITE IT: BIBLE VERSE

REFLECT: WHAT DOES THIS MEAN TO ME?

RESPOND: WHAT DO I SAY TO GOD ABOUT THIS?

REST IN MEDITATION: HOW IS GOD ASKING ME TO CHANGE?

Examen

1. Ask God to see your day and actions through His eyes
2. Thank Him
3. Review and meditate on your day and actions
4. Face your shortcomings
5. Ask God for guidance and pray about tomorrow

I'M THANKFUL FOR...

MY SINS & SHORTCOMINGS TODAY

Day 25   *Morning Prayer*

O Jesus, through the Immaculate Heart of Mary, I offer You my prayers, works, joys and sufferings of this day for all the intentions of Your Sacred Heart, in union with the Holy Sacrifice of the Mass throughout the world, in reparation for my sins, for the intentions of all my relatives and friends, and in particular for the intentions of the Holy Father. Amen.

READ & WRITE IT OUT: BIBLE VERSE

REFLECT: WHAT DOES THIS MEAN TO ME?

RESPOND: WHAT DO I SAY TO GOD ABOUT THIS?

REST IN MEDITATION: HOW IS GOD ASKING ME TO CHANGE?

Lectio Devina

1. Ask God to see your day and actions through His eyes
2. Thank Him
3. Review and meditate on your day and actions
4. Face your shortcomings
5. Ask God for guidance and pray about tomorrow

I'M THANKFUL FOR...   MY SINS & SHORTCOMINGS TODAY

Examen

Day 26   *Morning Prayer*

O Jesus, through the Immaculate Heart of Mary, I offer You my prayers, works, joys and sufferings of this day for all the intentions of Your Sacred Heart, in union with the Holy Sacrifice of the Mass throughout the world, in reparation for my sins, for the intentions of all my relatives and friends, and in particular for the intentions of the Holy Father. Amen.

READ & WRITE IT: BIBLE VERSE

REFLECT: WHAT DOES THIS MEAN TO ME?

RESPOND: WHAT DO I SAY TO GOD ABOUT THIS?

REST IN MEDITATION: HOW IS GOD ASKING ME TO CHANGE?

Lectio Devina

1. Ask God to see your day and actions through His eyes
2. Thank Him
3. Review and meditate on your day and actions
4. Face your shortcomings
5. Ask God for guidance and pray about tomorrow

I'M THANKFUL FOR...   MY SINS & SHORTCOMINGS TODAY

Examen

Day 27   *Morning Prayer*

O Jesus, through the Immaculate Heart of Mary, I offer You my prayers, works, joys and sufferings of this day for all the intentions of Your Sacred Heart, in union with the Holy Sacrifice of the Mass throughout the world, in reparation for my sins, for the intentions of all my relatives and friends, and in particular for the intentions of the Holy Father. Amen.

READ & WRITE IT OUT: BIBLE VERSE

REFLECT: WHAT DOES THIS MEAN TO ME?

RESPOND: WHAT DO I SAY TO GOD ABOUT THIS?

REST IN MEDITATION: HOW IS GOD ASKING ME TO CHANGE?

Lectio Devina

1. Ask God to see your day and actions through His eyes
2. Thank Him
3. Review and meditate on your day and actions
4. Face your shortcomings
5. Ask God for guidance and pray about tomorrow

I'M THANKFUL FOR...

MY SINS & SHORTCOMINGS TODAY

Examen

Day 28   *Morning Prayer*

O Jesus, through the Immaculate Heart of Mary, I offer You my prayers, works, joys and sufferings of this day for all the intentions of Your Sacred Heart, in union with the Holy Sacrifice of the Mass throughout the world, in reparation for my sins, for the intentions of all my relatives and friends, and in particular for the intentions of the Holy Father. Amen.

READ & WRITE IT: BIBLE VERSE

REFLECT: WHAT DOES THIS MEAN TO ME?

RESPOND: WHAT DO I SAY TO GOD ABOUT THIS?

REST IN MEDITATION: HOW IS GOD ASKING ME TO CHANGE?

Lectio Devina

1. Ask God to see your day and actions through His eyes
2. Thank Him
3. Review and meditate on your day and actions
4. Face your shortcomings
5. Ask God for guidance and pray about tomorrow

I'M THANKFUL FOR...

MY SINS & SHORTCOMINGS TODAY

Examen

Day 29

O Jesus, through the Immaculate Heart of Mary, I offer You my prayers, works, joys and sufferings of this day for all the intentions of Your Sacred Heart, in union with the Holy Sacrifice of the Mass throughout the world, in reparation for my sins, for the intentions of all my relatives and friends, and in particular for the intentions of the Holy Father. Amen.

READ & WRITE IT OUT: BIBLE VERSE

REFLECT: WHAT DOES THIS MEAN TO ME?

RESPOND: WHAT DO I SAY TO GOD ABOUT THIS?

REST IN MEDITATION: HOW IS GOD ASKING ME TO CHANGE?

Lectio Devina

1. Ask God to see your day and actions through His eyes
2. Thank Him
3. Review and meditate on your day and actions
4. Face your shortcomings
5. Ask God for guidance and pray about tomorrow

I'M THANKFUL FOR...

MY SINS & SHORTCOMINGS TODAY

Examen

Day 30

Morning Prayer

O Jesus, through the Immaculate Heart of Mary, I offer You my prayers, works, joys and sufferings of this day for all the intentions of Your Sacred Heart, in union with the Holy Sacrifice of the Mass throughout the world, in reparation for my sins, for the intentions of all my relatives and friends, and in particular for the intentions of the Holy Father. Amen.

READ & WRITE IT: BIBLE VERSE

REFLECT: WHAT DOES THIS MEAN TO ME?

RESPOND: WHAT DO I SAY TO GOD ABOUT THIS?

REST IN MEDITATION: HOW IS GOD ASKING ME TO CHANGE?

Lectio Devina

1. Ask God to see your day and actions through His eyes
2. Thank Him
3. Review and meditate on your day and actions
4. Face your shortcomings
5. Ask God for guidance and pray about tomorrow

I'M THANKFUL FOR...

MY SINS & SHORTCOMINGS TODAY

Examen

Day 31   *Morning Prayer*

O Jesus, through the Immaculate Heart of Mary, I offer You my prayers, works, joys and sufferings of this day for all the intentions of Your Sacred Heart, in union with the Holy Sacrifice of the Mass throughout the world, in reparation for my sins, for the intentions of all my relatives and friends, and in particular for the intentions of the Holy Father. Amen.

Lectio Devina

READ & WRITE IT OUT: BIBLE VERSE

REFLECT: WHAT DOES THIS MEAN TO ME?

RESPOND: WHAT DO I SAY TO GOD ABOUT THIS?

REST IN MEDITATION: HOW IS GOD ASKING ME TO CHANGE?

Examen

1. Ask God to see your day and actions through His eyes
2. Thank Him
3. Review and meditate on your day and actions
4. Face your shortcomings
5. Ask God for guidance and pray about tomorrow

I'M THANKFUL FOR...

MY SINS & SHORTCOMINGS TODAY

PRAYERS & REFLECTIONS ON YOUR SPIRITUAL JOURNEY THIS MONTH

Patience

IS ADJUSTING
YOUR TIME TO

God's time

MOTHER ANGELICA

O Blood and Water,

which gushed forth from the Heart of Jesus as a fount of Mercy for us, **I trust in You!**

(St. Faustina's Diary, 84)

Start Being Brave About Everything

Saint Catherine of Siena

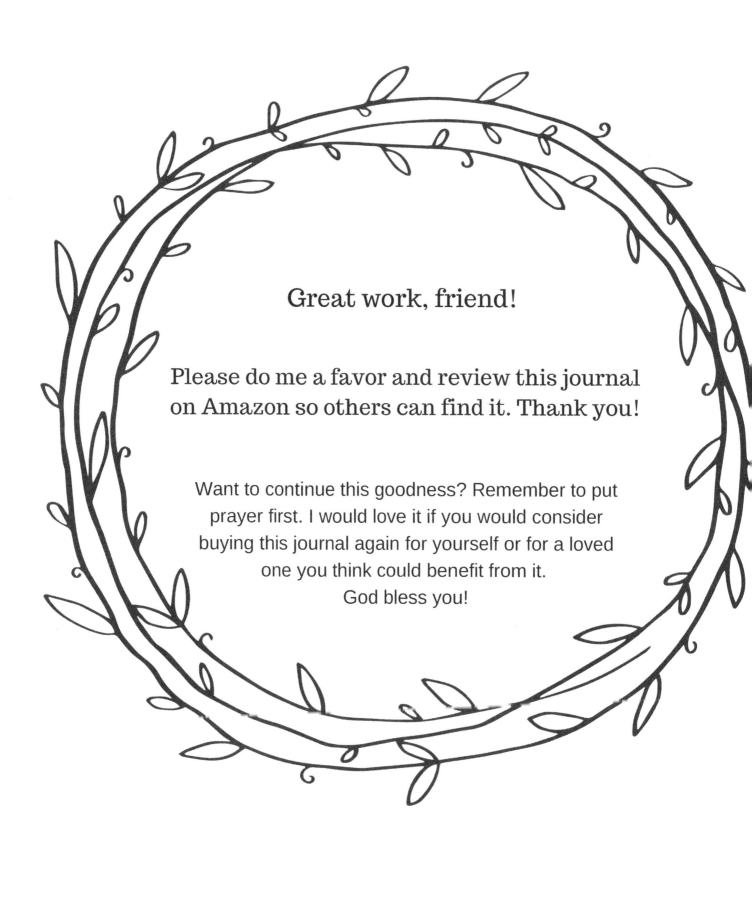

Great work, friend!

Please do me a favor and review this journal on Amazon so others can find it. Thank you!

Want to continue this goodness? Remember to put prayer first. I would love it if you would consider buying this journal again for yourself or for a loved one you think could benefit from it.
God bless you!

Made in United States
Orlando, FL
23 September 2024

51827735R00117